PUNCH
ON SCOTLAND

PUNCH
ON SCOTLAND

Edited by Miles Kington

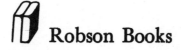 Robson Books

A PUNCH BOOK PUBLISHED IN ASSOCIATION
WITH PUNCH PUBLICATIONS LIMITED BY ROB-
SON BOOKS LIMITED BOLSOVER HOUSE 5-6 CLIP-
STONE STREET LONDON W1P 7EB © 1977 PUNCH
PUBLICATIONS LIMITED.

First impression 1977
Second impression 1980
Third impression 1984

ISBN 0 86051 002 6

Printed in Hungary

Contents

Introduction

Not long ago I was chatting to a Scottish cartoonist about the possible changes that could come about in a post-devolution Scotland, and suggested that there might be a move to change the Bay City Rollers to the Bay City Reelers. He flew into an unexpected rage and grasped me by both lapels. I thought, reasonably, that he was protesting about the sheer feebleness of the joke. Not so.

"Why is it that the English simply have no idea of the way the Scots live?" he stormed at me. "When will you get it into your thick heads that 99% of the inhabitants have never danced a reel in anger, have never seen one danced and would be quite happy if they went to the grave without ever being involved in a reel, foursome, eightsome or otherwise? There's only one kind of foursome the Scots are interested in, and that takes place on the golf course."

To put it another way, the Scots can get pretty touchy about English attitudes. They hate the stage props with which they have been equipped by Sassenach legend—the knobbly Harry Lauder sticks, the white heather and sporran, the hoots-mon-the-noo imitations, the what-is-worn-under-the-kilt inquiries, the caber and bagpipe jokes. They loathe being typed as haggis-eaters. Most of all, they hate the idea, wherever it came from, that Scots are a mean penny-pinching race who reach some kind of national peak of parsimony in Aberdeen.

So, as this volume consists largely of English attitudes to the Scots, I shall have to tread very carefully. Let me say at the outset that I know that nobody wears the kilt any more except in parts of Edinburgh, Perthshire and New Zealand. That the national dish of Scotland is not haggis but the fish supper. That tartan is most often found adorning football supporters' tammies or the beer cans in their carry-outs. That the Scots, far from always drinking whisky neat, often mix it with lemonade. And that most Scots do not live up glens or on isles but deep in cities.

The trouble about this stripping away of clichés is that what is left underneath is a declaration that the Scots are not so very different from other people, and where's the humour in that? Luckily, the Scots *are* different from other people. Ask any Scot. Better still, ask several Scots. They will tell you in great detail what is special about Scotland. Unfortunately, their answers will differ greatly depending on whether they come from Edinburgh or Glasgow, the town or country, the Highlands or Lowlands, depending on whether they are exiles or stay-at-homes, Puritan or liberal, mad or indifferent about football, nationalist or internationalist, drunk or sober.

Leave the Scots alone and they splinter immediately; the only thing that unites them deeply is the auld enemy, England.

So there is this to be said for English attitudes to Scotland, that as soon as you skirt the dafter identikilt images you do find general truths about the Scots that the Scots might not admit themselves. (A good many Scots have confessed in confidence to me that they would never dream of returning to live in Scotland, but it took Dr Johnson to say out loud that the best view in Scotland was the high road to England.) And nowhere is this truer than in the pages of Punch. Over the last hundred years Punch has published hundreds of cartoons about Scotland, thereby chronicling changing English attitudes to things Scottish, and you will find many unexpected things among them, together with the quite predictable grouse moor and ghillie jokes.

You will find, for example, that many even of the grouse moor jokes are anti-English with the hapless Southern tyro, not the wily ghillie, being the butt of the cartoon.

You will find a true reflection of the way Scots are capable of both Puritan discipline and complete excess, though usually it comes in reverse order with great drinking on Saturday and a grey silence on Sunday. Statistically it has been shown recently that the Scots do get drunk more often than other Britons, but they were getting drunk more often in Punch cartoons eighty years ago than any other nationality, as indeed they were also going to the kirk more often.

You will find faithfully recorded the way the Scots, though infuriated by the kilt and sporran image, are quite happy to surround themselves, and fill their shops, with Bonnie Prince Charlie driving gloves, thistle-shaped corkscrews, tartan lavatory covers and cuddly Loch Ness monster dolls.

You will find equally faithfully reflected the Scottish obsession with certain sports (golf, football and English-baiting), their curious ability to joke about death, and the exotic rhythms and vocabulary of their native speech. (It is said, for example, that Charles Keene would never finish a Scottish joke until he had consulted a Scottish expert as to the right phrasing and spelling. And his best-known one, "Bang went saxpence" was no invention but a directly recorded piece of conversation.)

Which brings us to the vexed question of Scottish meanness. I say "vexed" for one very curious reason. This is not the first book devoted to Scotland by Punch; it is the fourth. *Mr Punch in the Highlands* appeared at the end of the last century. It was closely followed by *Mr Punch's Scottish Humour,* and rather more leisurely pursued by *Mr Punch in Scotland* at the end of the 1920s. Now, you might suppose that the first, cruder collection of Scottish jokes was full of cartoons about Aberdeen and meanness. Far from it. There is scarcely a whisper in it to suggest that any Scotsman had ever done a mean act. The second book has a modest share of meanness jokes, but it is not until you reach the third and most modern that you find a real flood of them.

So, as cartoonists are rarely known to avoid milking a common humorous topic, this suggests very strongly that the myth of Scottish meanness had not even taken root eighty or ninety years ago, but that soon afterwards it had already become a familiar stereotype. No-one knows for sure where it came from (several writers in this book advance their own theories, all different) but there was a suggestion in a recent work on Scottish humorists that Punch and Punch alone was responsible for the fashion, and that *Bang went Saxpence* started it. In other words, that this magazine is to blame for one of the worst libels ever committed against an entire nation.

Should I rather belatedly apologise on behalf of Punch? I think not. Certainly one should apologise for the sheer *badness* of so many jokes about Aberdonians and other Scots tarred with the same brush. And yet it is true also that while the Scots often display great generosity and openness, they can at the same time in their usual contradictory fashion act with extreme, let us say, carefulness. They are not ashamed either to borrow jokes from the despised English, even about the very same mythical meanness; Chic Murray's piece in this book kicks off with a gag which you will find elsewhere in a cartoon at least fifty years earlier, and indeed some of the cartoons in this collection represent the first appearance in print of jokes which have become classic gags since, with their origin often forgotten.

In the period covered by this book Scotland has tended to attract more artists in the early days, and more writers in modern times, which is no bad thing considering that artists drew better then and writers write better nowadays. You won't find much about Scottish politics in 1900, nor much about deer-stalking in 1977, but otherwise writers and artists have returned to the same general themes over and over again. That is why I have split the book into sections covering the same area—so that the reader can among other things trace the evolution of the English view of Scotland. (As a gesture to humanity I have included no Loch Ness jokes.)

Many Scots readers will conclude, no doubt, that English views on Scotland show no development whatever over the last century. That is as it should be. If there is one thing the Scots hate more than being misunderstood by the English, it is being understood by the English. They are a proud people and do not wish to have their true nature guessed at by such a stolid nation as the English. I only hope this book contributes a little to the great tradition of misunderstanding which has always bound our two great countries.

MILES KINGTON

Chapter One

Aberdeen and all that: the great Scotch myths

As explained in the introduction, there seems no reason for calling the Scots or the Aberdonians mean, any more than for thinking the Irish stupid or the Italians cowardly. Nevertheless, the myth of meanness did ride strong for a while and produced some enduring humour, so it seems silly to ignore it completely, especially as Scots comedians have themselves made good capital out of it. In this section, three of today's more celebrated Scots comedians take a look at this and other Scottish myths, with a full supporting cast of wrong-headed cartoons and articles.

"It states quite clearly on the invitation ticket, McFarlane—*evening dress!*"

12

There was a Scotsman,
a Scotsman, and a Scotsman . . .

Stanley Baxter

WE should, of course, have taken a taxi. But we hadn't and we couldn't find the Drake Room at 71 E 56th Street. "I'll ask this chap," said Tom, "Excuse me, could you tell us how to . . ."

"Beat it, ya punk," said the large rumpled New Yorker without moving a muscle of his parchment-covered po-face. The mingling of hurt, bewilderment and shocked incredulity on Tom's face was an unforgettable sight. The incident was the main talking-point for him and his brother Jack—the Scottish Alexander Brothers singing act—for the rest of the North American tour.

Not because Tom may have been mistaken for a mugger or a panhandler but because the man had been wantonly and grossly rude. Nothing appals a Scot more than gratuitous rudeness. For my fellow-countrymen are the most sensitive, the most sympathique and the most sociable people in the world.

As a result they are terribly vulnerable to the unsociable and the uncouth. Watch a Glasgow tourist, say, being snubbed by a reserved Londoner and you'll see a picture of pathetic red-faced chagrin. We like to mix and be mixed with. Mr. Powell rants in vain as far as Scotland is concerned. Black people awe and fascinate us and we like them. It's never occurred to us to have a colour bar. And we're not virtuously self-conscious about the absence of race prejudice.

Americans impress us and we're as sociable as hell with them. We still hark back to the heart-warming wartime statistic that some ninety per cent of US servicemen chose to spend their leaves in Scotland.

We appreciate our Indian and Pakistani grocers and busmen. I was interested to hear a Scottish bus conductress chatting cosily with her driver. "I'm tellin' ye, Mohammed, there's nae Christian charity about yon fella at a'!" A lesson in unselfconscious integration.

We get on famously with the provincial English but with the Southern English ... Ah, the Southern English. What to Scottish ears are upper class accents and the loud confident, at times imperious, voices make many Scots feel socially inferior—much as Robert Burns felt in those Edinburgh drawing-rooms where a guid Scotch tongue was considered vulgar and everyone was frantically trying to acquire a horrid bool-in-the-mooth English accent.

In Scotland any English man or woman who isn't Cockney (The BBC has taught us the difference between posh and non-posh) is apt to be considered something of a toff.

But except in Perthshire where most of Scotland's Southern-educated aristocracy and sundry old school tycoons are entrenched there's little class-consciousness in our country.

Only in the bigger hotels is "sir" (or "sur") heard. The Scot visiting London is surprised at how often he hears the word. It embarrasses him.

I'm always delighted on returning to Glasgow to experience the sturdy class-lessness of its natives. You can be as aristocratic-looking and as well-groomed as Sir Alec Douglas Home, but that won't stop a lorry-driver leaning out of his cab and bawling at you, "Am I oan the right road tae Auchenshuggle, Jim?" Or the small shabby recidivist, Scotticè "wee bachle," confronting one with the question, "Huv ye got the time oan ye, Mac?"

My native Glasgow, I'm happy to say, is stiff with friendly forthright characters. My especial joys are the waitresses in the smaller eating places. I show them off with pride to unsuspecting English visitors and other foreigners who penetrate the fastnesses of Lowland Scotland. If you are wise enough to reciprocate their mateyness you discover that the ministrations of these delightful ladies can be almost embarrassingly slavish.

"Don't take the soup, dear," one of them whispered confidentially in my ear the other day, "It's rotten!" Later she showed equal solicitude when she brought me a pot of tea on a soup plate. "Watch this pot, son," she warned, "I've pit it oan the plate because it's leakin'." Then again came the confidential whisper. "The miserable bastards will no' buy ony new teapots."

It's a mark of favour if the waitress addresses you by your first name. In one Sauchiehall Street restaurant I used to drop into the fairly-regulars at the table included an accountant, lawyer, Foreign Office bigshot on leave, a TV journalist and a successful business man. All worthy chaps and the waitress favoured us all. No one, of course, dreamed of objecting to what permissive Londoners, in their Victorian way, would have regarded as "undue familiarity." She overheard someone congratulating the lawyer on being able to stick QC after his name. "Aye, he's aye been 'QC' . . . 'quite cocky'!" she said. Then with affection she declared, "Ach but ye're no' a bad fella, Jim."

The legend that Scots are mean originated with Sir Harry Lauder when he was a low comedian before becoming "that grand old minstrel" as Churchill had it. Because of the awful image of the Scot Lauder gave the world his memory is not exactly revered by many. The smear of meanness has become a crashing bore to millions of Scots who never saw Lauder. The painful truth is that the Scot can be stupidly generous and the most oft-used sayings in Scottish pubs are—"It's MA round," "I'm on the bell" and the more aggressive, "Ye're havin' a double!"

Also detested are those scabrous appelations we've had to put up with for years—"pawky", "dour" and, most hated of all, "canny." The revolt against over-Scottishness has been going on for some time, ever since Glaswegians flocked enthusiastically to "Hair" at the Metropole Theatre and to the Close

Theatre Club for a basinful of the avant garde.

One great Scottish idiosyncrasy remains with us—the intense amusement we get out of the subject of death. Tell a joke in Cockney on a Scottish stage and you will meet with a deathly silence, the icy non-reaction that made the Glasgow Empire a'house of despair for many English comedians. But get on to the subject of death and the audience becomes alive.

The great Glasgow comedian-actor Jack Radcliffe was famed for his death-bed scenes. No man died more amusingly on the stage. Scots still remember the sketch in which he incurred the wrath of his wife by announcing that he felt a little better. "Too late!" ran her imperishable line, "I've just bought in two pun' o' bile't ham for the mourners." Another well-loved classic was Jack's portrayal of the dying shipyard worker surrounded by his greedy family. "You'll get a thousand Tam . . . There's a thousand for you, Lizzie . . . And Andra, ma eldest son, you'll get two thousand." The tag-line—he was talking in rivets.

Another of our comedy stars, Alec Finlay, has delighted thousands of Scots at home and all over the world with his undertaker sketch. "The corpse looks very well, Mrs. McGrundy. He's got a grand suntan." "He *should* have! He's just spent twenty poun' on a holiday at Dunoon!"

Why this delight in death? Possibly a mass reaction from the grim all-black solemnity of lengthy Scottish funerals. With cremation our funerals are usually much shorter now. Alas, this may result in the death of our beloved death-fun.

Stout Person. "Any use trying to borrow a fiver off you?"
Scot. "Ay, the exercise will do ye guid."

Great Strength returns the Penny.

There was a Scotsman . . .
(Part Two)

by Chic Murray

WHAT is a Scot? This is the question people keep asking me. I can only say that a Scot is a man who keeps the Sabbath, and everything else he can lay his hands on. Joking apart—is the Scot really mean? Are all these stories about Aberdeen true? Well, you can judge for yourself, my father was an Aberdonian, and a more generous man you couldn't wish to meet. I have a gold watch that belonged to my father, he sold it to me on his death bed . . . so I wrote him a cheque.

Is the Scotsman's thriftiness hereditary? Maybe the story of my uncle can help to answer this question. An American lady in hospital once needed three blood transfusions to save her life, and my uncle, being the unselfish man that he is, volunteered to be a blood donor. For the first pint she gave him fifty dollars, for the second pint she gave him twenty-five dollars, and for the third pint . . . nothing! So you see, it's in the blood. When I was a kid, my mother hired a woman to push my pram, and I've been pushed for money ever since.

Please don't think we are all just money grabbers in Scotland. We realise that money isn't everything, women are the other five per cent! After all, what is money. The Mint makes it first, and we've got to make it last. The Scot is not as tight-fisted as some people make out. I read in a newspaper only last week where a Scotsman had offered £50,000 to the first man to swim the Atlantic in gumboots. In business, the Scot has few equals; my father once told me that my grandfather was one of the most successful men in Britain, so much so that one businessman in London wrote to him asking the secret of his success. My grandfather wrote back and told him it was all a matter of brain food, and that he would give him a correspondence course at two guineas per lesson. Each week my grandfather sent him a pair of kippers, which cost him 2s., for which he received two guineas by return. About six months and forty-eight guineas later, he received a letter which read . . .

Dear Mr. Murray,

I have had a feeling for some months now that two guineas is rather a high price to pay for a pair of kippers. I am now almost convinced that the charge is much too heavy.

But my grandfather was equal to those aspersions . . . He wired back . . .

"CONTINUE COURSE, UNDOUBTEDLY BEGINNING TO SHOW RESULTS."

Of course, thriftiness is not the only characteristic that the Scot has to take a bit of stick for. Take the kilt, for instance. He is very proud to wear the kilt and display his clan tartan. But he's all too often the butt of the alien. I wore my kilt only last week down south, in enemy-held territory, and was approached by the usual inquisitive young lady, who wanted to know the age-old secret. I thought, "Here it comes again." She said, "Pardon me Mr. Murray, but my friends and I would like to know, what is worn under the kilt?". . . I said, "Madam, nothing's worn, everything is in good working order" . . . I think it's time we did something about this question, could see-through sporrans be the answer? Just a thought.

One cannot mention the Scot without mentioning whisky, the national drink. There are only two rules for drinking whisky. First, never take whisky without water, and second, never take water without whisky! The Scot is very proud of being able to hold his drink. I remember being out with a friend of mine one night, and we had a real ball. The next morning I met him, I said, "You had a real skinful last night, did you manage to get home all right?" He said, "I was getting home fine when that big policeman tramped on my fingers" . . . Then there was the Scot in London on holiday, who had been out on a binge and was making his way home, when he was set upon by a gang of thugs . . .

The Scot, a born fighter, and with whisky courage, put up a very stubborn resistance, but after a long and bloody struggle, he was finally over-powered. The gang leader, after such a struggle, was expecting a rich booty, but after turning his pockets inside out, he found only sixpence. He said "Sixpence, only sixpence after a struggle like that" . . . his mate said, "Maybe we're in luck, can you imagine what it would have been like if he'd had a shilling!"

Still Scotland has much to recommend it; for instance, we gave the world golf. St. Andrews is the home of golf, but I'm sure St. Andrew never played it or he'd never have been a Saint. I don't like to boast, but I'm a very accurate golfer myself, straight down the middle, that's me. It will give you an idea of how accurate I am when I tell you that last week I lost my first ball in ten years—the string broke. I was taught golf by an old Scottish professional, a real purist, everything had to be done according to the book. I'll never forget my first morning I went out on the tee. He gave me a seven iron, I was so nervous I could hardly hold the club. He placed the ball on the tee, taking my courage in both hands I swung at the ball, and to my amazement it flew through the air right on to the green and rolled into the cup. I stood there waiting for congratulations. He said, "Naw naw, laddie, that'll no' do ata'. You're using the wrong grip . . ." Now, what else do we have to blow about in Scotland . . . The bagpipes. What else? Many a hungry garrison has been relieved to hear the bagpipes . . . In the distance, but so many people can't stand them, so where does a piper learn to play? I remember, I took up the bagpipes once. I was blowing away merrily and marching round the room, when my wife came upstairs. She said, "You'll have to do something about that noise," but what could I do? I took my shoes off and marched around in my stockinged feet—you've got to come and go.

Well, I hope I have enlightened some of you foreigners who have been reading this. Remember that Scotland has produced many things to make this a better world to live in. She gave the world chloroform invented by Simpson—Television, invented by Baird—Penicillin invented by Fleming, and Funnyosities invented by Chic Murray, what more could you ask? . . . In answer to that last question,. please send on a Rolls-Royce Silver Phantom, 1970 model, and in return, I will write on a plain postcard, a minimum of twenty words telling you exactly why I like it!

PS In case of fire, cut round dotted line.

COMMERCIAL INSTINCT

Dugald. "Did ye hear that Sawney McNab was ta'en up for stealin' a coo?"

Donald. "Hoot, toot, the stipit bodie! Could he no bocht it an' no paid for't?"

Highland Wedding

"Just think, lass, Robbie Burns died
in this very bed."

"You almost forgot the buttonholes."

"Aye, I'll think about it if ye' throw in the lectern."

There was a Scotsman . . .
(Part Three)

by Jimmy Logan

I HAVE often been asked if there are any major differences between Scottish and English humour. Well, it is interesting that to the Scot a funeral is a humorous subject, whereas the Englishman can see no laughter whatsoever on such a sad occasion.

On the other hand, the Englishman thinks that the Vicar is an extremely funny person and can be so portrayed on stage in any farce, almost by tradition. The Scot must not laugh at the Minister.

Funerals: imagine an old couple sitting by the fire; he is puffing away at his pipe and she is knitting. We can hear the ticking of the clock, breaking the silence. She looks up and says:

She: What are you thinking John?

John: Oh, I was just wondering.

She: What were you wondering John?

John: Well, when the time comes, and we have to be parted, I was wondering what to put on your tombstone.

She: Oh, that's easy, just put wife of the above.

From the world's point of view, the humour of the Scot ends at the image of Sir Harry Lauder. Harry Lauder first appeared without a kilt, singing an Irish song, about 1890. At that time Scottish comedians toured America and Canada, bringing a breath of Scotland to the emigrants. By the time Lauder made his first American tour, he was firmly established as a Scottish entertainer throughout the British Isles. His personality and his great ability in showmanship soon caught the imagination of the American public. He would make a point of having his name called by the bell boy in every American hotel he stayed in and would publicly tip the boy with a penny or a signed photograph of himself; he was in fact the original Jack Benny.

The meanness of the Scot, perpetuated by Sir Harry Lauder, originated in Aberdeen. The meanness of the Aberdonian stems from the fact that Aberdeen as a city was one of the few cities, if not the only in Britain, to declare itself bankrupt. The City Fathers, in their wisdom, decided around the year 1795 that they would design a main street in Aberdeen, second to none. Union Street was born. A forerunner to the present town and country planning, the city was magnificent. Unfortunately, the finances that were to be obtained from the surrounding feus were not forthcoming, and so, in 1817, Aberdeen as a city declared itself in a state of bankruptcy. This went on until 1822 and so the story was born that the Aberdonian was not too keen to pay for anything. A typical example of this can be found, to this day, on the sea-side post card with a photograph of the famous Union Street, empty, with the sign reading "Aberdeen on a flag day."

The Scot does not regard himself as a mean man, indeed anyone who has travelled north and experienced Scottish hospitality will, I am sure, agree with this; but he is regarded as "canny." By tradition it is a country of men of independence who dislike being obligated to any person and to whom being in debt is considered a great shame on the family. The thrifty Scot made his mark on the world's jokes. This pride and his independence made other nations feel that he was money-conscious, but it is completely unjustified. Rumours of financial meanness were started by Scots who have been making money out of them ever since.

An example: one enterprising reporter discovered that an elderly gentleman in the Highlands had amassed a fortune, reckoned to be worth £1,000,000. The reporter travelled north and discovered the millionaire living in a very plain, simple cottage. It was dark when he knocked at the door. Eventually the door opened and there stood the millionaire himself with a candle in his hand, to light the way. "Come in, come in," he said, for the Scottish reputation of hospitality is an important one. They sat down in the small front room, the candle between them. The old Highlander eyed the young reporter.

Reporter: I would like to find out how you managed to amass such a fortune.

Highlander: Certainly, I would be delighted to give you some words of wisdom, do you have to take any notes?

Reporter: No, I'll keep them in my head.

Highlander: Good, in that case I can blow out the candle.

In the history of this country, when the battle was at its worst, when the cause was lost or seemed to be so, the Scot could always find something to laugh at. In the dark days of 1940, the name Dunkirk was featured on the front page of every British newspaper. A cartoon was published, showing two Scottish soldiers reading the latest news with the headline BRITISH ARMY LEAVES DUNKIRK. One Scot said to the other, "You know, Willie, if the English give in we might have a bit of a fight on our hands."

There are Government bodies working at this moment extremely hard to bring industry to the Highlands. Whilst not wishing to deprecate their efforts, I would suggest there is a dividing line between bringing industry to the Highlands and industry to the Highlander, who prefers, if possible, a life that has still an air of tranquillity. One recent visitor to the north of Scotland was a Spanish gentleman who found the beauty of the islands and the nature of the Highlander fresh and invigorating. One Highlander said to him, "I notice that you keep using the word *mañana:* what does it mean?" "Ah," said the Spaniard, "*mañana* means tomorrow, next day, next week, next month, next year, sometime into the far unforeseeable future." "Ah," said the Highlander, "we have no word in the Gaelic for anything as urgent as that."

Scottish humour is a limitless subject, but inevitably reflects very much the characteristics of the people and the feelings of the country. The humour of the Glaswegian is legendary. He is no respecter of persons or state and considers that Glasgow was originally built on the site of the Garden of Eden. In fact it comes as a surprise to him to discover that others may disagree with his point of view. The Glaswegian in his cups has a sense of humour second to none and he is very proud of his birthplace. A visitor waiting at a bus stop found beside him, for example, a middle-aged Glaswegian, slightly swaying, but contentedly eating his fish supper, one of our great national dishes. The Glaswegian eyed the obvious foreigner and leaning on his shoulder said:

Glaswegian: I'm from Glasgow.

Visitor: Good.

Glaswegian: Glasgow's the greatest city in Scotland.

Visitor: Quite right.

Glaswegian: Glasgow's the greatest city in Britain.

Visitor: I quite agree.

Glaswegian: Glasgow is without a doubt, the greatest city in the whole world.

Visitor: Without a doubt.

At this, the wee Glasgow man turned and began walking away:

Visitor: Where are you going?

Glaswegian: To think up another argument.

Edinburgh humour, on the other hand, is based on the city's being class-conscious, ie, Edinburgh is renowned for fur coats, fish and chips and pianos. Edinburgh has the reputation of being the windiest city in the world. No matter where you travel, you can always tell an Edinburgh man. When he walks round a corner, he by instinct holds on to his hat. The Glaswegian is not readily accepted in Edinburgh and I consider it one of my greatest accolades when I first appeared in that city, the father of a friend of mine turned to him and said, "Where does Mr. Logan come from?"—"Glasgow," said his son with some trepidation. "Is that so," said the father, "he could almost be an Edinburgh man."

It is still my belief that the best of humour stems from life and life is rich in Scotland. I can still see my grandfather sitting in his chair after he and my grandmother had celebrated their sixtieth wedding anniversary. Grandfather was wearing a hired dinner suit, black boots, he still had his cap on, rosy cheeks, snow white moustache and a very wilting carnation. He looked up at the mantelpiece to the trusty old clock, "What time is it?" he said. "It's eleven o'clock, grandad." "Oh, that's a pity," he said, "I was just going to go out and get you all fish suppers." The picture in my mind of grandad standing in a queue at the chip shop, in his dinner suit, his flat cap, boots and his wilting carnation will live with me for many years to come.

A famous Scot once said, "I'd rather be hanged in Scotland, than die a natural death anywhere else in the world." The old Victorian image of Sandy and Mac with the moths flying out of their sporrans is dead. Or is it, I wonder? Maybe with this new generation we have still retained some of the warmth and character of the old. The end result is a mixture that must retain all the best ingredients of personality and individuality in a world where these are sadly disappearing.

Lowlander. "Third return tae Inverness."
Ticket-clerk. "Change at Aberdeen."
Lowlander. "Na, na! I'll tak' ma change here—Ah've bin tae Aberdeen."

Scottish Dog Day Afternoon

in which DUNCAN CAMPBELL lets the side down by revealing
what a hash his fellow Scots make of organised crime

AT the end of 1975, a young Frenchman called Raymond Burles walked into a bank in Marseilles and held the employees at gun point while he collected £2,300 in francs. He slipped the notes neatly into a small black leather case. On top of the money he placed his automatic pistol. Then he zipped the case up. The bank manager and a customer grabbed him and he is now in jail. Very Inspector Clouseau, very French.

But it would be wrong, in this Year of Devolution, to award the top marks for Imaginatively Bungled Bank Robberies to the French. Scotland has them beaten, gloves down.

When the Army of Provisional Government, the tiny Scottish paramilitary independence movement (if movement is the right word for four men who will spend the next few years inside Barlinnie Jail) decided to carry out a fund-raising bank job, they did it with considerably more flair.

They met on a Tuesday lunchtime 1975, in a Glasgow pub near their chosen target. With a couple of pints under their belts, they drove off to the bank in a van they had hired, in their own name, from a firm in Perth. Only to find the bank, as W. C. Fields found Philadelphia, closed.

Back they went to the pub, imagining that the bank was just shut for the lunchbreak. A few pints on, and they returned to find a man leaving the bank and locking it behind him. This branch, he explained courteously, had been closed for months.

Where was the nearest one? they asked. Just down the road, he told them, pointing in the direction of a prefabricated temporary bank. But their arrival there coincided with that of a visiting Securicor van and they drove off in search of a third.

No Securicor men around and, even better, it was open for business. Parking the van in a narrow cul-de-sac, they burst in with a shotgun and began the raid. All went well, although one of the men caught his hand briefly in the grille, and the four retreated to discover that carrying out a three-point turn with a large van in a small cul-de-sac is not the easiest of manoeuvres. Particularly when you are trying to make an escape from the scene of an armed robbery and the name of your van-hire firm is boldly lettered on the side of your getaway vehicle.

"Ah, well," as they say in Scotland, "they ken noo."

Also kenning noo are the three men who carried out a raid on the Royal Bank of Scotland in Rothesay, a holiday resort on the Isle of Bute.

The raid started, Glasgow High Court was told, with one of the men getting stuck in the bank's revolving door and being helped free by staff. Having made it inside, this raider asked one of the tellers for £5,000, explaining that they were going round the world and, if she wanted, she could come with them. Mrs Elspeth Ritchie (25) was not interested. The man then suggested that £500 would be sufficient. Again she refused. This process went on until Mrs Ritchie turned down a final compromise suggestion of 50p.

"What if I shoot you?" asked the robber.

"Go ahead," replied Mrs Ritchie.

At this point, a second raider vaulted the grille only to fall flat on his face beside La Ritchie. £600 was gathered but on the way out the team again got stuck in the revolving door, pushing it frantically the wrong way. It may be some small consolation that the doors in Scotland's prisons are of a simpler design.

No such tactical problems faced a Mr Andy Mackay during his performance at an Edinburgh bank in 1972. He was a 42-year-old Post Office worker of "previous good character" and he was not, as he pointed out at his trial, greedy.

All he required of the bank teller was for her to fill up a small paper bag with money. To this end he arrived at the bank with two radio batteries wired together which, he explained quietly, was a bomb that would explode unless she filled up the bag. He apparently expected her to stuff it full of oncers and send him on his way. Instead, she dipped into the £100 denominations and he departed with £6,000.

Flummoxed, Mackay leapt into a taxi, which stopped at the traffic lights, leapt out of it and off to the Channel Islands where he was picked up three weeks and £4,500 later.

How, asked his advocate, did he manage to spend it all so quickly? Ah, said Mackay—when he wanted a bottle of champagne he would fly to Paris and buy one. If Sunday afternoon promised to be dull, he would fly to Madrid and watch a bull-fight of which there are a scarcity in the Edinburgh region. Ah, said the judge—six years.

The taxi is but one means of inspired getaway. Another original one, the bicycle, was employed one Christmas when a freelance Glasgow bank-robber headed off with just over £2,000 from a Milngavie bank. Being slightly drunk, he fell off as he tried to mount and was helped astride it by two sympathetic workmen. They were rewarded with £200 each. He was arrested later that evening in the pub almost directly opposite his front door. The workmen were never seen again but are doubtless always on hand whenever anyone is having difficulty in mounting their bicycle.

Another escape route employed after a robbery at a St George Cross bank in Glasgow was the city's underground. But since there is a choice of only fifteen stations and the line runs in one small circle, this proved to be a Bad Idea. After two spins on the circuit, the fugitive gave himself up.

The same inventiveness comes through even when a Scot is south of the border. Stephen Callaghan was out of work and out of money in Luton in 1975 and wanted to return to his native Dumbarton. He spent his last £2 on a bottle of sherry and a toy gun, and marched into a newsagent.

"This is a stick-up," he told the girl behind the counter.

She failed to understand his accent so he pulled out the toy gun and said "Bang Bang."

"You're dead," she replied.

He tried the same approach on a cafe with an equal lack of success. On that occasion he explained: "I'm not joking." Again the assistant laughed at him.

His third attempt was in another shop. There the cashier told him to "push off." Callaghan grabbed the till and was grabbed himself by two assistants. "This is the third store I've tried," he said. "And all they've done is laugh at me."

Sentencing him to two years probation, Judge Robert Lymbery told him: "There is one main factor in your favour. As a criminal you are thoroughly incompetent and not, I think, a potential danger."

So, when talk turns to preservation of law and order throughout the world, let no-one forget that Scotland's bank robbers have done more than almost anyone else to ensure that crime does not pay. If Patty Hearst had been a Scots girl, the Symbionese Liberation Army would have been routed years before.

Householder. "An' whit are ye wantin' at this time o' nicht?"
Mendicant. "Will ye no give me fourpince for a bed?"
Householder. "Bide a wee and I'll come doon an' tak' a look at it."

The Decay of the Kilt

Mr. Briggs loquitur:

I AM going down to Scotland, to the country of the kilt,
For a little salmon-stalking in a place they call Glen Tilt;
And as I always like to be a Roman when at Rome,
I've purchased the correct costume and it has just come home.

The kilt is most becoming, and it hangs with grace and ease,
Though perhaps a little draughty in the region of the knees,
And if there should be midges—but no doubt the Scotch are drest
In the clothes Experience has found to suit the climate best.

The dirk that dangles from my waist looks very *comme il faut,*
And the sporran in my stocking gives a finish, don't you know?
The girls are all in raptures as they gaze at me in turns,
 And mother says they'll take me for another Robert Burns.

Sandy loquitur:

Oh, mony are the fallacies that Ignorance'll breed,
An' mony the mistakes a man 'll get intil his heid,
But the maddest o' delusions mad wi' which some folks are fillt,
Is that ye suld gang tae Scotland, gin ye want to see the kilt.

For a' the year I hevna seen a single kilt but ane—
A wee bit white-legged Coackney wha' was trudgin' through the rain;
The water it was pourin' owre his knees intil his shoes,
An' eh! but he was wishin' for a pair o' honest trews.

Na! gin it's kilts ye're wantin', dinna win sae mony miles!
Jist bide at home in Lunnon toun and gang tae Seven Dials,
An' there amang the coasters, hurdy-gurdies, dancin' bears,
Ye'll fin' yer bogus Scotsmen pipin' bogus Scottish airs.

Volumes of Trouble

DUNCAN CAMPBELL

"DO you know what fluxions are?" I inquired, glancing up from the magazine I was reading.

"For fluxions," replied Alister Macalister, "you have to see infinitesimal calculus, and I have never seen it, because I am confined for my general information to fal-fies."

" 'Fal-fies'?"

"Outside of fal-fies," said Alister, "I am what you might call an ignorant working man, but inside of that I have more knowledge than a university professor."

He left the room and returned with a bulky volume entitled "Purdie's Encyclopaedia," Vol. V.—FAL-FYZ.

"I plough right through her every winter," said Alister. "She was gifted to me by Sandy Drumshaw.

"It happened like this," he went on. "When his Aunt Martha died Sandy got her bookcase; and one morning when he was going down to Glasgow to sell a cow he said to his wife, 'I think we should get some books for our bookcase.'

" 'That is just what we should dae,' says Mrs. Drumshaw, who was an Ayrshire woman. 'And get big yins, Sandy, because it is a big bookcase.'

"He saw from the papers that there was an auction sale to be held in a house in the suburbs, and after a lot of walking he found the place. It was the big house of a wealthy business gentleman who made his money by always going bankrupt. In one of the rooms Sandy got his eye on a pile of strong hefty-looking books, and he just waited beside them until the auctioneer came into the room, followed by a crowd of wild fat women and two or three shabby wee men.

" 'Now,' says the auctioneer at last, 'what am I offered for these ten volumes of "Purdie's Encyclopaedia" on the table over there beside the gentleman from the Highlands?'

" 'Half-a-crown,' roared Sandy at the pitch of his voice, putting the fear of death into all the fat women.

" 'Gone for half-a-crown,' says the auctioneer, thinking no doubt that it might be as well to get rid of a fierce wee chap like Sandy as soon as possible.

"Sandy was so proud of his smart work that he was outside the front gate before he realised his circumstances. It took all the strength of his arms to hold up his books, and he was loaded with them from his waist to the point of his chin. He had also a long white beard and a nasty cold in the head.

"There was a policemen standing there and a man leaning against a barrow.

"Says Sandy to the man at the barrow, 'How much would it cost to carry these books to the nearest tramway car?'

" 'Half-a-crown,' says the man.

" 'That is as much as the books themselves have cost me,' says Sandy, very indignant.

"Then he went up to the policeman, and says he, 'How far is it to the nearest tramway car?'

" 'There are no tramway cars or buses allowed within two miles of this district,' says the policeman. 'We are most terrible exclusive.'

" 'What am I to do?' says Sandy, with his voice getting very weak. 'I have to catch the train for Auchterbrose.'

"The policeman looked at Sandy's beard flowing over "Purdie's Encyclopaedia," and says he, 'I believe if you could find a circus you might get taken on as a representation of Niagara Falls.'

"This brought on one of Sandy's sneezing fits, and in two shakes his books were scattered all over the road.

"However, the policeman was a decent young fellow and he loaded Sandy up again. 'Now', says the policeman taking him by the shoulders and turning him round, 'if you go straight along in that direction you will be all right.'

"But Sandy got so dizzy with exhaustion and discomfort that he could not keep himself from turning round corners, and at last he bumped into a big red-faced man.

" 'I am sorry,' says Sandy, 'but I did not see you.'

" 'That is all right, comrade,' says the man. 'Have you got a boil on the back of your neck?'

" 'I have not,' says Sandy. 'It is my beard that is caught between two of my books. I wish you would get it out for me.'

" 'Purdie's Encyclopaedia"?' says this chap. 'These books are of no use to you at all, comrade. Have you read "Das Kapital"?'

" 'I have not,' says Sandy. 'These books are not for reading; they are for the bookcase.'

" 'You must read "Das Kapital" at once,' says the red-faced man, 'and learn all about Socialism.'

" 'I do not want to learn about Socialism,' says Sandy; 'I am a Conservative. Can you tell me if I am near the tramway lines?'

"The wild fellow glared down at Sandy. 'Are you prepared to die?' says he in a terrible tone of voice.

"Sandy staggered back and his books crashed to his feet, 'Are you threatening to murder me?' says he.

" 'I am putting a case,' says the Socialist. 'Are you prepared to die with no provision made for your wife and family, who would starve under the present capitalist system?'

" 'There is always plenty of provisions in my house for my wife and family,' says Sandy. 'If you threaten me any more I will call a policeman.'

" 'Policeman!' roars the Socialist. 'We are going to have all the policemen hanged from the lamp-posts, and you along with them, you dirty little scab!'

"Sandy picked up one of his books for self-defence and looked round for a policeman, but in the feverish condition he was in he seemed to see nothing but lamp-posts, and he took to his heels and bolted for his life, leaving all the rest of "Purdie's Encyclopaedia" behind him.

"He came round to see me the next night and presented me with the book. He told me he could not bear the sight of it. 'Me and the wife have decided, Alister,' says he, 'that we will just use the bookcase for keeping the dishes in.' "

Super Scot. "So ye're an Aberdonian, are ye? From all I hear they're a thriftless lot in Aberdeen."

And of course, the wonderful world of Scottish souvenirs

Annual Sale

After the summer season, the Tartan Trinket Board announces a grand auction sale to clear stocks. The main lots are listed below; a full catalogue is available on request

★350,000 clan maps of Scotland, with Campbell and MacGregor mistakenly transposed and Forsyth in the North Sea.

★A selection of fragments from the North Inch at Perth. (This is slightly shorter than the English inch, and comes cheaper.)

★40,000 small models of Scotsmen in kilts. When the kilt is raised, it reveals a huge pair of tartan underpants with the inscription: "Now ye ken!"

★20,000 packets of shortbread, mistakenly labelled "A Gift Frae Auld Hong Kong."

★A huge range of car key-rings, driving gloves, thermos flasks, dangle dollies etc., all exact replicas of those used by Bonnie Prince Charlie on his historic motor tour of Scotland.

★One meat pie, hardly used. Could be warmed up, or used as door-stop.

★Black Watch car rugs, as used in two World Wars and Edinburgh Tattoo.

★40,000 flasks of ancient Celtic after-shave lotion, made by hand in remote factories on the fringes of Paisley.

★300 chinaware haggis replica money boxes, with free give-away ½p piece already inside!

★Discontinued foreign-produced line of Argyll and Sutherland Highlanders dolls with slant eyes and yellow skin.

★30,000 volumes of Sir Walter Scott's Waverley Novels, as second-hand. Could be sold separately for reading, split up to form libraries or purchased in one lot as barricade for street-fighting. Slight mildew on one copy of *Ivanhoe*.

★John Buchan's "Thirty-Seven Steps"—special offer.

★1,500 gaily woven, thick, durable, woolly facsimiles of Landseer's *Monarch of the Glen*. Just right for those long, chilly summer evenings.

★60,000 boxes of Edinburgh Rock in sixty-four different fluorescent shades. Could be eaten or would make scale model of Edinburgh Castle.

★75,000 tartan-lined wooden caskets decorated with an eagle's claw in tasteful fibreglass and a sprig of heather; when the claymore handle is lifted it plays the opening bars of the Skye Boat Song. Ideal for keeping Scottish souvenirs in.

★Assortment of hard-wearing odds and ends—broken oatmeal biscuits, pieces of Arthur's Seat, sprigs of lucky grey heather and what we think are miniature cabers.

32

Grand Tour of the Greater Scottish Delusions

In which PATRICK RYAN takes a swift Baedeker around the jungles of the Celtic id

AFTER seeing the Trossachs, Loch Ness, John o' Groats, Sauchiehall Street on a Saturday night and both the Inner and Outer Hebrides, the indomitable tourist should next proceed on the official conducted tour of the Greater Scottish Delusions. Although the tour can be started almost anywhere on the gloomier side of Hadrian's Wall, it is usually commenced in Edinburgh where the party leaves Waverley Station by the front door and turns left along Princes Street to sample the Incredible Tartan Delusion.

It will be immediately noticed that the shops are principally stocked with gentlemen's skirts, bobbled berets, tea cosies, golf-club helmets and other Hong Kong gew-gaws made of worsted cloth woven with alternate stripes of hectically coloured warp and weft to form varying chequered patterns. Because of the neolithic simplicity of this tartan weave, the Scots infer that each garish patchwork comes down from time immemorial and represents the textile insignia of a particular clan. Those brave enough to brush aside the romantic cobwebs have discovered, however, that the patterns were mostly invented in the early nineteenth century by Sir Walter Scott, one Stewart of Garth, and ambitious tailors anxious to make themselves a few thousand bawbees. The main impetus to this Delusion came in 1822 when George IV visited Edinburgh and suggested that Scotchmen attending his functions should each wear their respective family tartans. This announcement led overnight to the invention of a large crop of primeval tartans and any dignitary short of criss-cross imagination soon found a tailor only too eager to provide him with a family design. Inventiveness has never since slackened and when duty requires the Duke of Edinburgh to wear a kilt of historic Balmoral tartan today, he may be comforted to know that its black, red and lavender check was personally designed by his preceding Prince Consort, Albert the Good.

This Laughable Cult of the Kilt is a further sartorial example of Scottish self-deception. In persevering with this impractical and uncomfortable masculine petticoat, the Scots are the last remaining human species to consider the male knee as a sexual attractant. Perhaps even an erogenous zone to strictly brought-up Presbyterian ladies. The kilt is ritually worn by many in the mistaken belief that it is the traditional garment of ancestral clansmen. Whereas cooler historians hold that it was actually invented in the early part of the 18th century by a Mr. Rawlinson, a Sassenach Quaker who came to Invergarry to set up as an iron smelter. Bonnie Prince Charlie, though imaginatively depicted therein, sensibly never wore a kilt in his life till the Battle of Culloden, after which he had to adopt the draughty tutu while hiding from his hunters. The kilt is highly unsuitable for he-men striding over moors because its flare permits tall heather to make improper advances and the knees get painfully chapped in inclement weather. As Queen Victoria noted to her distress when they once had to get the doctor to John Brown because her faithful whisky-carrier could barely walk for his "dreadfully lacerated and swollen knees caused by the flapping of his sodden kilt".

And the Mother of the Empire was doubtless equally unamused by the unjustified family attribution of Edinburgh's Spurious Royal Mile. This seventeen hundred and sixty yards of tatty buildings and humdrum shops running down to Holyroodhouse has as much regal bearing about it as the shabbier end of the Old Kent Road, and the Scottish Tourist Board could likely be sued for misrepresentation under the Trades Description Act. Providing one of our actual living Royals doesn't get in first and have somebody in the Tower for taking their name in fraudulent vain.

The masochistic tourist who ill-treats himself to such perambulation will be able to store up further future punishment by buying a tinned haggis at a wee grocer's shop along the way. The Scottish mind is inhabited by the Peculiar Haggis Hallucination which leads the sufferer to believe that this flaccid lump is his native ambrosia, whereas its recipe openly proclaims it to be a type of Boiled Butcher's Dustbin. The Scots make haggis from those intimate parts of animals which all other nations but the vultures throw away. Finding that they could sell all their guid meat at high profit to the English, they forced the remnant offal on their own stomachs, thus making a national delicacy out of an economic necessity. To perpetrate a haggis, you chop up a sheep's entrails with onion, suet and oatmeal, mix with nutmeg, lemon-juice and stock, cram the resulting sad splodge into the animal's paunch, stitch up and boil for three hours. The outcome is a sort of Offal Steamed Pudding, which looks like a pale castrated bagpipe, tastes like savoury cardboard, and is monstrously productive of the wind.

The Scots coax this unhappy concoction down their gullets with tastebud-numbing libations of whisky, a form of booze in which they take an unwarranted proprietorial pride in the grip of their Great Whisky Romance. As its maiden name, usquebagh, indicates, the hard stuff was actually invented by the Irish, who brought its secrets over to Scotland when they first colonised the place and weaned the inhabitants off their regular diet of human flesh. The self-trumpeted Scotch genius for making whisky is actually a matter of fortunate geology. The productive areas just happen to possess an abundance of spring water that passes through red granite before percolating peat moss and providing a liquid ideal for distilling the best poteen. Until about eighty years ago, Scotch whisky wasn't much imbibed outside the country. Brandy was the

gentleman's drink elsewhere and the English only took to drinking Scotch when the phylloxera epidemic cut off supplies of French cognac at the end of the nineteenth century.

Northward where the natives make the single malts, the diligent tourist will have opportunity to observe directly the Myth of the Proud and Independent Highlander. Much blame for this illusion can be allotted to Sir Edwin Landseer and other Victorian artists of the glen-and-ben school who painted shaggy landscapes of unnaturally purple heather inhabited by shaggy aggressive cattle and shaggy kilted Highlanders. Robert Burns, who knew a thing or two about his fellows, reported finding nothing up north but "Highland greed . . . Highland pride and Highland scab and hunger". A modern journalist echoed him when describing Highland education as "learning to work with subsidies". And the present Highlander is renowned among public servants as the ultimate pastmaster of the British Isles at obtaining government hand-outs, social security benefits and any available form of municipal charity.

In addition to the haggis, the Scots exploitation of the sheep also brings pain to the rest of mankind with their Extraordinary Bagpipe Trauma. The bag is made out of a sheepskin, the pipes of cocoa wood and ivory, and the resultant sound is like a clarinet with strangulated hernia. Rabid though the Scots pretend to be about this painful ullulation, its instrument of emission was not of their invention. Connoisseurs of musical arson will know that the bagpipes were introduced into Britain by the Romans as the *tibia utricularis*, which was the favourite instrument of Nero and likely the one he was playing when Rome frizzled, rather than the gentle violin. The bagpipes are today very popular among the medical profession in Scotland, probably because their operation is reminiscent of playing music on a set of human intestines.

And the final feature of this package tour of the Greater Scottish Delusions is the Fantasy of the Canny, Honest, Imperturbable Scot, which figment is locally regarded as symbolising the Scottish National Character. Whereas, in actuality, the majority of Scots are feckless, unable to hold their drink, and voluble till the cows consider emigration. Kipling did much to foster this Delusion by his depictions of imperturbable Scots ship's engineers who, with the bridge waistdeep in water, would puff their pipes impassively and say, "Dinna fesh yersel', skipper, the boilers'll nae blaw up the nicht and the auld tub'll see us all hame tae Greenock". But, on the more recent judgement of one of their own Members of Parliament, Mr. Joseph Grimond, they are more realistically dubbed as "bickering, garrulous toadies" with marked streaks in their national character of veniality, irascibility, and windbaggery. The Chief Constable of Barcelona can testify to the aluminium self-control of visiting Scots, supported by the senior magistrate of Glasgow who lately suggested that cattle trucks would be more appropriate transport for Scottish football fans than railway carriages. And the hopeful Mr Wayne Harbin of Marathon Manufacturing will be able to comment later on their native honesty when he wakes one day to find the whole fabric of his first Clydeside oil-rig has been steadily knocked off and flogged piece-meal to scrap metal dealers.

And so, with the sun setting like a glorious clockwork orange, we bid farewell to the primitive beauty of the Greater Scottish Delusions and leave the wee, slickit, cowering, timorous Scotchman ever haunted by that national sense of insecurity which requires regular assurance from the rest of us that his brain is the canniest, his landscapes the bonniest, his breeks the brawest, and his knees the loveliest of them all.

Sister (to elderly prodigal who is much given to pawning his things). "What's this ticket on yer best coat, Sandy?"
Sandy. "That was the nicht I was at McPhearson's ball, they tack yer coat from ye at the door, and gie ye a ticket for't."
Sister. "H'm—aye—I see there's yin on yer troosers as well."

The Short History of Scotland

Scottish History was a simple game for any number of clans. The object of the game was to beat the English and there were three main rules. One: to confuse the English, always fight among yourselves at the crucial moment. Two: to confuse the English, always claim a crushing defeat as a romantic landmark of history. Three: to confuse the English, always give people and things at least two different names.

The Romans had always believed that the world ended at Northumbria until Hadrian made an expedition further north. He returned with the news that the world did indeed end at Northumbria and built a wall as a warning to unwary travellers. The Scots, coming from Ireland, saw it merely as another English trap and crossed it in droves, except on Sundays. (The real Scots were Picts.)

This beautiful thing shows the high standard of craftsmanship brought to whatever it is by whoever built it. It may well be a weapon of some kind or perhaps just left lying around to confuse the English. The Dark Ages were hardly noticed up north—it got a little gloomier, perhaps—and the Scots had no time for Hastings; Macbeth was too busy killing Duncan and Malcolm was too busy killing Macbeth (or Maelbeatha).

The first man to startle the Scots by actually beating the English was Robert Bruce (or Brus), who came from a Norman family. His decisive victory in 1314 kept the marsh of Bannockburn in Scottish hands for ever, or until the 1330s. But by dying at the age of fifty-three and leaving a five-year-old heir, he started a tradition of plunging the country into chaos which finally culminated in the all-time record of . . .

. . . James V (or James 0 of England) who died less than a week after his daughter, Mary Queen of Scots, was born. Our picture shows her practising golf (or gowf), a game invented by the Scots in which the man with the lowest score won. This confused the English. Mary's relations with men, many of them her husbands, cannot be mentioned in a family magazine, but she promptly abdicated in the approved style as soon as her son (VI and I) was a year old.

Catastrophe struck in 1603 when James became King of England. For almost a century the fight against England seemed pointless, though the Protectorate did give the Scots a chance to chalk up several thrilling defeats, and they spent most of their time moodily engaged in religious schism. Their demoralisation is shown by the fact that Charles II (above) was Charles II of England *and* Scotland.

At last the Stuarts (or Stewarts) fled from England and Scottish History could start again. The Massacre of Glencoe was a complete success—with the death roll at about forty, it may be the most famous massacre per fatality in history. The '15 was a washout—the Old Pretender arrived too late for the best defeats—but in the '45 the Young Pretender was a smash hit from the finish.

James Watt (or Wha?) spent much of his working life among steam engines and we show here the historic moment when he proved that by use of the same principles you could make a pretty good cup of tea. Other notable Scottish inventions of the time include the kilt (by Sir Walter Scott), Sir Walter Scott (by George IV) and bad Scottish ballads (or third degree Burns).

As Scotland has not been invaded or defeated by England in modern times, Scottish History can be said to have come to an end, though there have been half-hearted attempts to see Scotland's perpetual failure in the World Cup as a romantic tragedy. The Scot is now a quiet kilted gentleman dreaming of past disasters in the hillsides. The English who go to Scotland may be confused to find that no one there wears a kilt, but the English have always been easily confused.

39

Friend. "And what if you *have* lost a shilling on a horse?"
Scott. "It isna only masel'. There were sax of us in it."

Chapter Two

Huntin', Shootin' and Fitba': Sport, the Great Divider

There seem to be three kinds of sporting activity in Scotland. There are the lairdly pursuits which involve the mass slaughter of birds, animals and fish. There is golf. And there is football, which is also a branch of religion. They hardly overlap at all.

In addition, there are Highland games, which remain incomprehensible to most southerners. In his diaries, Evelyn Waugh relates that he attended a Highland meeting which was a lamentable failure; not a single competitor managed to overturn the caber. No-one seems to have explained to the benighted Waugh that the whole point of caber tossing was to land it as near as possible upright on its end. From the sound of it, he attended a particularly good session.

Cricket was introduced to Scotland by the British soldiers holding the Scots patriots* captive after the '45, but it has never really caught on. This is probably just as well. If Scotland ever beat England in a five-day Test, the ensuing celebrations would be horrific to behold.

*(or rebels.)

MORE FOOTBALL RESULTS

Jock. "Th' Sco'sh ha' woon, lassie."
Jean. "So I see!"

Modest but unsuccessful tyro (who has been flogging the river four hours).
"Is there anything I am omitting to do, MacWhirr?"
MacWhirr. "I wadna just say that exactly. But I'm thinkin' ye drink varra leetle whusky for a man whae's no killin' fush."

Glesca Fitba'

[Based on an advertisement eight inches long inserted by the Police in the Glasgow Press prior to a Glasgow Cup Tie (Rangers v. Clyde), giving "Directions for the preservation of order at the above Assemblage," including instructions about the routes to be followed by rival Brake Clubs, and a warning as to the carrying of "Flags, Banners, Rattles, Whistles or other noisy instruments."]

PETER, his head heavily bandaged and his left arm in a sling, limped in and called on the barman for "some o' the stuff thae Yankees wid gie their Statue o' Liberty for."

"Jungs!" cried McNidder, "whaur hae ye been, Peter? Ah thought a man o' your age wid ken enough tae gang straight hame efter payin' aff frae a seeven-months' voyage."

"Ah dae, an' Ah did," Peter replied solemnly. "This is no' the result o' a nicht wi' auld King Alcohol. Hae ye ever been tae a league fitba' match, McNidder?"

McNidder opened his eyes very wide.

"Ay, ye may weel stare. Spendin' yer spare time, as ye dae, sailin' model yachts, ye hae nae idea o' whit goes on at a first league match.

"If ever ye tak' yer mind aff the trum o' yer wee boat's sails on a Setturday efternoon an' gie a thought tae a nobler pastime like fitba', ye probably imagine there's naething in it but twa elevens on the field an' a few thoosan' spectators watchin' them play, an' applaudin' whiles when yin o' the teams scores a goal? Ye're mebbe saft enough tae think a man can come hame frae his work, wash his face, change his claes an' simply set oot for the match?

"Ye'd be wrang, McNidder. Ah thought the same masel' wance, but it's no' so easy as a' that. Efter ye've got on yer guid claes ye fill hauf o' yer pockets wi' big stanes, and the rest wi' bottled beer. (The stanes keep ye in ammunition until ye hae emptied the bottles.) Then ye get oot yer rickety—a rattle, ye ken, yin o' thae things that mak' a terrible row when ye whirl them roon'—an' try it tae see its lungs are a' richt, so tae speak. Finally ye get yer wee flag oot the umbrella staun', an' ye're equipped for the match."

"Whit's the wee flag for?"

"It's yer club colours, an affshoot o' the school tie; an' the stick comes in handy, forbye; a' members o' a brake-club cairry them. Of course ye hae tae be a member o' a brake-club or ye're nae lover o' sport. When ye're a' ready ye jine the brake at the prearranged rongdevoo an' awa' ye go.

"In the early days, afore the thing wis reduced tae a fine art, the brakes made their way tae the fitba' ground by ony route they liked, wi' the result that the sportsmen dissipated their energies afore they got there, fechtin' runnin' duels wi' rival brake-clubs while the harmless citizens took refuge in shop-doors an' behin' lamp-posts an' pillar-boxes, tae escape the flyin' missiles.

"The polis hae things properly organised noo. Wan route is laid doon for wan club's supporters, an' anither for the ither club's. In this way the public are oot o' danger provided they hae the sense to use a third route; an' besides that the brake-clubs arrive at the ground wi' practically a' their ammunition an' their fechtin' qualities unimpaired.

"Ah forget the name o' the lad that said, 'Ma country richt or wrang,' but that's the way it is wi' thae brake-club fitba' enthusiasts, only their club's never wrang. They don't care which team wins as lang as it's their team. They ken whit a sportin' instinct is. Let the players get on wi' the game, they say, an' we'll bash up the ither club's supporters, if we've got tae kill hauf the ither spectators first. An' Ah'll say this for them, they cairry oot their part o' the programme.

"Ah hear tell the polis are gaun a step further, an' are stoppin' them taking flags an' ricketies intae the ground. If they dae, it'll save some o' the fitba' clubs a wheen o' money. Ah believe they were contemplatin' getting captive balloons for the supporters that wanted to see the game withoot riskin' their lives."

"Losh, Ah'd no idea it wis as bad as that!"

"It's worse than that," said Peter. "Hauf o' the brake-club members don't ken wha's won till they read the sportin' editions at nicht, and the ither hauf get the result in the hospital or frae a friendly bobby in the polis-station."

Just then the carpenter of Peter's ship came in.

"Hullo!" he greeted Peter; "they've let ye oot o' dry dock, hae they?" Turning to McNidder he added, "Man, Ah never thought Ah'd see Peter alive again when that sea washed him aff the poop on tae the efter well-deck."

"Ye're an awfu' liar, Peter," said McNidder reproachfully.

"Naething o' the kind. Ah never said Ah wis at a fitba' match. Ah wis only tellin' ye whit they're like in Glesca."

Scots Mother (to Grandfather). "The bairn ought to be at his books. Ye'll destroy his mind wi' yer freevolous goin's-on."

THE GAMES AT BRAEMAR

BILL TIDY previews one of Scotland's major industries

"Event 27. Cycle Race. 'DE'IL TAK' THE HINDMOST'.
Say, what does that mean, buddy?"

"C'mon, Scottish Office, Whitehall!"

"Quickly, Andy, a bottle of porridge."

"You're in my toe holds, McPherson."

"Don't tell me, Alex. It's the prize winning
Benbecula British Legion Pipe Band."

To an Unknown Deer

OWEN SEAMAN

(Somewhere above the head of Loch Fyne)

KING of the treeless forest, lo, I come!
  This is to let you have the welcome news
That you will shortly hear my bullet's hum
  Shatter Argyll amid her mountain-dews;
Will hear, from hill to hill, its rumour fly
  To startle (if the wind be not contráry)
The tripper gathering picture-postcards by
  The pier at Inveraray.

This is your funeral, my friend, not mine,
  So play the game, for slackness I abhor;
Give me a broadside target, large and fine,
  A hundred paces off—don't make it more;
If in a sitting posture when we meet,
  You mustn't think of moving; stay quite steady;
Or (better) rise, and standing on your feet
  Wait there till I am ready.

Lurk not in hollows where you can't be found,
  Or let the local colour mock my search;
But take the sky-line; choose the sort of ground
  That shows you up as obvious as a church;
Don't skulk among your hinds, or use for scouts
  The nimble progeny of last year's harem
To bring reports upon my whereabouts
  In case I chance to scare 'em.

If I should perforate you in a place
    Not strictly vital, but from that rude shock
Death must ensue, don't run and hide your face,
    But let me ease you with another knock;
And if, by inadvertence, I contrive
    Initially to miss you altogether,
Stand till I empty out my clip of five,
    Or make you bite the heather.

As for your points, I take a snobbish view;
    I dearly love a stag of Royal stuff;
But, if a dozen's more than you can do,
    Ten (of the best) will suit me well enough;
As for your weight, I want a bulky beast,
    That I may win a certain patron's benison,
Loading his board, to last a week at least,
    With whiffy slabs of venison.

Finally, be a sportsman; try to play
    Your part in what should prove a big success;
Let me repeat—don't keep too far away;
    My distance is a hundred yards (or less);
So, ere the eager gillies ope your maw,
    I'll say, in tones to such occasions proper,
The while I drink your death in usquebagh,
    "He is indeed a topper!"

Novice (after futile efforts): "I'm afraid I'm a very poor golfer."
Caddie: "Ye're no' that yet."

Legs of Destiny

DUNCAN CAMPBELL

DURING a recent sojourn in a certain Scottish township I strolled out one day along what the townsfolk call the "Sooth Road." About half-a-mile from the town I caught sight of the figure of a little boy. His back was towards me and he was leaning against the low wooden paling that bordered the roadway. I went up to him and said, "Hullo, what's your name?"

"It's Peter Bogle," he replied, without disengaging his eyes from their contemplation of the southern horizon.

"And what are you doing here, Peter?"

"I've come oot all this road mysel'," he answered proudly. "This is as far as I can go the day. But every day after this I'm goin' oot more an' more. An' I'll keep goin' away, away, till—till I canna get ony further."

With a last long look in the direction of his future journeyings he turned and, relinquishing the support of the paling, took my hand.

"Will you take me back to the toon noo?" he asked.

"All right, Peter," I said. "I'm sure you must be tired."

"No, I'm no tired," said Peter indignantly. "It's just my legs that's sore."

I glanced at his legs and marvelled that he had managed to walk so far. They were painfully thin and fragile, and shaped like a pair of callipers.

"Would you like me to carry you, Peter?" I asked solicitously.

"No, ye'll no carry me," snapped Peter.

As a compromise I suggested that we should rest for a bit. Peter consenting, I sat down on a convenient pile of stones and he settled himself comfortably on my knee.

"My legs is always gettin' sore," he informed me. "Does your legs get sore when ye walk wi' them?"

Before I could reply he suddenly wriggled from my knee, walked to the middle of the road and began to punch the air like a pugilist.

"What are you doing, Peter?" I exclaimed.

"I'm practisin' to be a goalie," said Peter. "I'm goin' away along that road," pointing southward, "as far as Glesca. An' when I get to Glesca I'm goin' to be the Celtic's goalie."

He came back and got on to my knee again.

"My legs'll no get sore then," looking up at me earnestly, "because a goalie doesna need to run. A goalie just stands in the goal an' keeps the ball oot."

"That will be splendid, Peter," I said. "I'll come and watch you playing."

"I'll let you in for nothing," said Peter graciously. "An' then," he went on, staring along the road, "when I get a lot o' money for bein' a goalie I'll go to Australia in a motor, an' I'll shoot tigers."

"How many tigers will you shoot, Peter?"

"Maybe ten thousand," nodding his head determinedly. "I'll chase them wi' my motor."

After gloating for a while over the picture of ten thousand slaughtered tigers, Peter abandoned his motor-car and came home and joined the army.

"I'm no going' to be one o' the standin' kind o'sojers," he explained, with a resentful glance at his legs. "I'm goin' to be a general on a horse."

"And what will you do when you meet the enemy, Peter?"

"I'll cut his heid aff," said Peter viciously. "See," he cried excitedly—"there I'm goin' skooshin' doon the road on my horse, killin' everybody."

As we walked slowly homeward Peter continued to recite the endless legend of his adventurous future. It was a tale of appalling massacres. All who crossed his path were slain. His blood-thirstiness, indeed, was shocking, and seemed to be the outcome of a spirit of fierce rebellion.

Before we entered the town Peter paused and glanced backward. "I wish my legs didna get sore," he sighed, "because that's a terrible long road."

He guided me to his home, an old-fashioned house in one of the side streets. An elderly dame was standing at the door.

"Granny," cried Peter, "I've been away oot the road all by mysel'!"

"Ye wee rascal," said Granny, shaking her fist at him in mock anger. "Whit has he been tellin' ye?" she asked, turning to me.

I gave her a short account of my meeting with Peter.

"Ay," she said with a wise smile, "we would a' like to be big folk, but we canna get ony further than oor legs'll tak' us. That," pointing to a shop on the opposite side of the street, "is where Peter got his legs. An' that's a' the length his legs'll ever carry him. A hunner-an'-fifty years," she went on, "that shop has been in the family. Peter's legs are maybe no very much to look at, but they're just the richt kind o' legs for oor business."

I glanced at Peter. He was staring across the street with a look of mingled terror and malevolence. Suddenly he lashed out savagely with an imaginary sword. "When I'm a general on a horse," he said sullenly, "I'll come an' I'll knock the shop doon."

Incensed at this heretical declaration, his granny picked him up and carried him into the house.

And so I was left gazing pensively at the drab front of Peter's destined prison-house. The sign above the shop read: "John Bogle, Tailor and Clothier. Established 1776."

The Pupil: "What do I do now I've finished winding?"
The Instructor: "Climb up the rod and stab it."

Will Ye No Come Hame Again?

"Hey, amigo. You want old Rangers' banner? Folds down into eight-man tent!"

"Shut up and get in with this lot. There must be a drink at the end of it!"

"Why should we throw you out of this country, señor? For Celtic supporters this is nothing!"

"I'm not having you for a start. You were shouting for the home team!"

BILL TIDY follows Celtic and Rangers through Europe

"You're a fanatic, Willie. Stranded, and all you want to do is follow a crowd to another match."

"Keep at it, lads. It's better than walking home!"

"Always the same. The ones who bother to come back are the worst!"

WELCOME HOME WILLIE McDUFF
STRANDED 6 MONTHS IN MADRID

"You're bad news, Willie. Celtic lost at home today."

A New Scottish Anthem

The Chairman of BBC Scotland has called for the composition
of a new Scottish national anthem which can be sung at the
beginning of sporting events to counterbalance
"God Save the Queen" . . .

Now that the match is almost started,
　Now that the teams are on the scene,
Raise your voices in common purpose
　　—Drown the singing of "God Save the Queen"!
　　　We don't want a Sassenach song;
　　　We want something braw and strong,
　　　So we've brought our ain refrain along:
"I'm a' right, Jock, I'm a' right!"

Chorus
Stand up, stand up for Scotland,
　Stand up and wave the flag!
Pass round the flask of Teacher's
　And gie us another fag!

Oh, say can you hear the referee's whistle!
　Say, can you hear its silvery tone?
No, all I hear is the noise of Scotsmen
　　—The Hampden roar *v.* the Wembley groan!
　　　So wave your tammy in the tartan sea,
　　　Wave your scarf for the land of the free
　　　And make rude signs if you're on TV
"I'm a' right, Jock, I'm a' right!"

Chorus
Stand up, stand up for Scotland,
　Or fall down on the ground;
We'll hail the St John's stretcher
　The next time it comes round.

Does anybody here know what the score is?
  Does anyone give a damn!
All that matters is another chorus,
  Another meat pie and another dram!
    Fling yourselves intae the fray,
    Take another swig and sway, boys, sway,
    For Hogmanay comes every day!
"I'm a'right, Jock, I'm a' right!"

Chorus
Stand up, stand up for Scotland,
  Fling your empties straight and true,
But be sure to keep one handy
  —There's an awfie long queue at the loo.

Now that the game is over and done with,
  Now that we—or they—have won,
Let's go and paint the town bright tartan,
  The evening's work is no' begun!
    Dream teams to pick for the next World Cup,
    Fish suppers to eat, more heavy to sup,
    And tomorrow we'll feel like death warmed up
—"But I'm a' right, Jock, I'm a' right!"

Chorus
Drink up, drink up for Scotland,
  Raise high your cairry-oot,
Cry loud and clear, and full of beer,
  The old cry: "It's ma shout!"

So here's to the land that gave you whisky,
  Here's to the land that gave you rain,
Here's to the Sabbath and early closing,
  And the broken windows in the Glasgow train!
    What though the bars all shut at ten,
    Through evil laws made by Englishmen
    —My cairry-oot's full of cans again!
"I'm a' right, Jock, I'm a' right!"

Chorus
Throw up, throw up for Scotland—
  What if you're feeling rough?
Throw up! and damned be any man
  Who first cries "Haud—enough!"

                                    M.B.K.

"This is the life, eh?"

mike williams

Chapter Three

Death, Weather, the Sabbath
and other Scottish customs

"As dead as a Scots Sunday" was one of the hilarious catch-phrases of the late John Knox, a remarkable performer who regularly played to full houses; to this day the pubs in Scotland are kept closed in his honour on the Sabbath. Other things that happen traditionally on this day are post-mortems on Scotland's football failure, and rain. Rain happens on other days, of course, but on Sunday you can't get out of it into a pub. Only into a church. None of this is comprehensible to an Englishman, and nor is the Scots habit of laughing about funerals, so we shall hurry through this section as quickly as possible using only a few cartoons and no articles. Remember, by the way, that the word Scotch is never used except to refer to whisky, eggs and mist. There is no known reason for this either.

"An what for are ye wearin' yer blacks the day, Mr. MacTavish?"
"I was at the Baillie's funeral."
" 'Twill ha' been a gran' procession, likely?"
"Ay, but verra little enthusiasm."

English Tourist (in the far North, miles from anywhere). "Do you mean to say that you and your family live here all the winter? Why, what do you do when any of you are ill? You can never get a doctor!"

Scotch Shepherd. "Nae, sir. We've just to dee a natural death!"

Scottish Cabby (explaining historic landmarks of Edinburgh to American tourist). "Yon's the house o' John Knox."

Tourist. "Wal, who was this John Knox, anyway?"

Cabby (shocked). "Mon! Do ye no read yer Bible?"

"SCOTCH MIST"
"The rain seems to be clearing off at last, Sandy."
"Ay, I doot it's *threatenin' to be dry!*"

The Laird. "Now, who on earth might those people, be, Donald, dressed like tourists?"

Father (on way to kirk). "Stop, ye' whustlin', Angus. I'll no hae a Continental Sawbath here."

THE SABBATH

Tourist. "Beautiful day!"

Highlander. "Ay, but it's no the day tae be talking aboot it."

Juvenis. "Jolly day we had last week at McFoggarty's wedding! Capital champagne he gave us, and we did it justice, I can tell you——"
Senex (who prefers whiskey). "Eh——h, mun, it's a' vera weel weddings at ye-er time o' life. Gie me a gude solid funeral!'

"It's the way Angus would've wanted it."

Jean. "Awfu' guid acting, Donald."
Donald. "Ay, but awfu' baad behaviour."

Temperance worker (paying a surprise visit to the home of his pet convert).
"Does Mr. MacMurdoch live here?"
Mrs. MacMurdoch. "Aye; carry him in!"

Chapter Four

A Wee Dram

W. Gordon Smith, in *This Is My Country,* says that "Scottish humour is sardonic, more reductive than English humour, and capable of sustaining surrealist non-sequiturs that most strangers to it are unable initially to comprehend". This may explain an exchange I once had in a Glasgow bar. I was standing peacefully by when a man rushed in, drank a pint of beer and a stiff Scotch, then rushed out again.

"He took that quickly," I said to the barman.

"Aye," he said. "He has to be careful. He's driving."

The Scots like drinking a great deal. They also tend to fall over and/or be sick, though whether they really like doing this I have never been able to decide. It must have been going on for a long time, though, because as long as Punch has been printing cartoons about Scotsmen, it has been printing cartoons about drunken Scotsmen. On the whole, I approve; it is more fun getting drunk in the company of Scots than of other races. I know of one unsuspecting English author who went to have a drink in London with two Scottish writers (both, incidentally, featured in this book) and woke up *three days later* on Crewe Station without the faintest idea how he had got there.

"BACKSLIDING"

The Minister (reproachfully). "Ah, James! I'm sorry to see this! I thought you were a steadfast teetotaler!"

James. "Sho I am, sir. But I'm no a bigoted ane!"

TENACITY

First North Briton (on the Oban boat, in a rolling sea and dirty weather). "Thraw it up, man, and ye'll feel a' the better!"

Second ditto (keeping it down). "Hech, mon, it's whuskey!!"

The Clachan of Chagrin

J. B. NAISMITH

IT is a far cry to Glen Whusky, where the whaups are piping above the braes and maybe the pipes are braying above the whaups, but it was there that Famd Macandrew painted his masterpiece, and he will never paint again. I have known Famd since long ago, when he was rising to fame as a painter of cattle. A journal notorious for its misprints had described him as the "famd" animal-painter, and his friends adopted the nickname with delight, since it happened to comprise the initials of the one already settled upon him—Foot-And-Mouth Disease.

Famd's pictures sold like wildfire. His kine were admired by the million, but the educated few, including some well-advised millionaires, admired his grass more. The grass was wonderful. Sometimes it was violet and sometimes scarlet. It varied from vermilion to saxe, cocoa, rust and other modest millinery colours. After a successful sale he would use ultramarine for the grass and red for the town. He was one of that glorious band who see the object "as in itself it really is." Except the cattle—they were quite lifelike.

It was while wandering in search of the ideal cattle that he had never yet found that Famd stumbled by accident upon Glen Whusky on a braw evening and found them. After floundering all day through peat-bogs he had slithered down a corrie and landed in a wee clachan, and there were the kye in a bonny bit of meadowland, grand upstanding beasts. Glen Whusky is really a beautiful valley. There is a distillery at the top end and a spirit factory at the other, and in the middle a place where they make whisky.

Famd got lodgings with a decent body in the clachan and set out next morning with a fifty-forty canvas on his back. It lacked but a few days till sending-in day and it behoved him to be busy. It was a snell morning and his landlady made him take a wee something to keep the cold out. She said it was a half "chill," but it was more like a whole dose of influenza. As he was passing the place where they made it, a man came out and greeted him, and they fell a-talking about the bonny beasts. Famd was for on, but the man would have him in, and before he could say "When" he was looking into half-a-tumbler of pure delight.

When at last he got to the meadow he found that the composition of the picture was going to present some difficulties. The cattle would not keep still. They were sooming round in the air like a mirage and playing hide-and-seek up in the trees. Famd reasoned with them for long and pleaded for them to play the game and give him a chance. At last he lost his temper and set about them; but all to no purpose; so he sat down and cried. In the late afternoon the crofters came and carried him home; but they couldna catch the beast with the fifty-forty on its head.

The next morning Famd stretched a new canvas and set out. He walked smartly through the clachan, looking neither to right nor left. As he was passing the last house, a two-storey building, a little old man came out and stopped him, and asked him if he was Maister Macandrew the penter. Famd admitted the fact and the little man was delighted. He told Famd how he had seen a little picture of his in a Glasgow shop twenty years before and thought it was the bonniest picture that ever was. He had bought it and carried it home, and it was the pride of the Glen. Wad he come in and see it?

Famd stepped in; but he couldna see the picture at first for a half-tumbler of over-proof that was shoved before his face. Famd was for pushing it away, but he remembered in time that it is not a kind thing and it is not a good thing to refuse Highland hospitality. And in any case the man was a patron of Art.

When he got to the meadow Famd found his subject and sketched it in. He worked hard for a time, but the sun got that strong he had a throat like fire. He stepped over to the burn for a drink, but the water was drumly with the snow melting up in the moors. Further up on the far side was a but-and-ben, and to it Famd went and asked for a drink of water. The old body reached down a bottle from the shelf and poured out the best part of a tumbler.

"Water, I said," roared Famd.

"Watter, quo' he," says the auld wife. "Guidsakes, is the man daft? Wantin' tae drink watter in a heat like this? Ye'll kill yersel'. Here."

"For ony sake, wumman," says Famd, "put a wee drop water intill't."

The old body near dropped the glass.

"Pit watter intill't, quo' he," she cried. "Wha ever heard tell on't? Look ye, is there ony room for watter there? Ye can tak' it or leave it."

Not wanting to offend the old body, Famd took it. Then he went and sat down at his easel again, but the heat made him drowsy and he fell asleep. In the late afternoon the crofters came and carried him home and his fifty-forty on the top of him.

At seven o'clock the next morning Famd chapped at the door of the last house in the clachan, and the face of him was drawn and haggard.

"Maister McTonal," he said, when the door had been opened, "listen to me. This picture has got to go off wi' the carrier at half-past four the day. The crate's ready and addressed in Mrs. McDougall's back kitchen. It just wants packin' an' a wheen boards nailed on. The framer must have it tomorrow wet or dry. I am goin' to finish it the day wet or dry. I ask you, Maister McTonal, as a lover and a patron of Art, if anything should happen to me this day, will ye see it off?"

"I wull," said Mr. McTonal. "Step inbye for a meenit an'——"

"I will not," said Famd, and fled.

At eleven o'clock the picture was more than half done. Famd was laying down his palette to light a cigarette when a deep voice behind him said, "It will pe a graund success whatever," and Famd, turning, saw an enormous gamekeeper with enormous dogs.

"It will pe the graundest picture I have ever seen," he said slowly, gazing at it. "It will pe for sale at Edinburgh?"

"Ay," said Famd.

The keeper slewed round his game-bag and drew therefrom a flask about the size of a hot-water bottle.

"We wull tak' a drop to bring success for it," he said.

"I canna, I canna," cried Famd, but something in the man's look stopped him.

"Ye canna what?"

"I canna finish that shadow to ma liking," said Famd.

"This will help ye," said the keeper, pushing the bowl into his hand.

After Famd had got it down somehow the man solemnly drained a dishful himself and strode off without another word.

Famd was resolved to get the thing done before the heat and burden of the day. The cattle were completed to his satisfaction, and the braeface beyond. There wanted but the foreground to be put into order. With his collar loosened and his mouth wide open to cool his throat, he carefully carried the easel, inch by inch, nearer the tree, so that he could lean against it. Then, seizing his brush, he stirred up a fine mixture on the palette, and, after one hour of glorious life and inspiration, with the old hills rolling round him in fantastic dance, he finished the picture. In the early afternoon Mr. McTonal took it and packed it up. Later on the crofters came and carried Famd to his rooms in the clachan.

For some time after he returned South, Famd kept his bed, troubled with sciatica. On varnishing day he went out for the first time and down to the Gallery. His picture had pride of place in the centre of the line, and in front of it Famd fell on the floor and was carried out by his fellow-artists, a broken man. In that last hour of frenzy at the foreground he had painted the grass green.

LIFE IN SCOTLAND

The Duke of Edinburgh sat down to salmon and carrots yesterday, flanked by white and coloured athletes. *(The Scotsman)*

Will the party responsible for the removal of a telegraph pole from opposite the Free Church, Callanish, please return same, as it was the property of my late brother.—Annie MacInnes. *(Stornoway Gazette)*

"Eh, but I had a rare t͟ e last year-r. A was at ma cousin MacWhuskie's a whole
forrtnicht, an' A didna once ken A was theer!"

A DISAPPOINTING HOST

Sandy. "A'm tellt ye hev a new Nebbur, Donal'."

Donald. "Aye."

Sandy. "An' what like is he?"

Donald. "Weel, he's a curious Laddie. A went to hev a bit talk wi' him th' ither
Evenin', an' he offered me a Glass o' Whuskey, d'ye see? Weel, he was poorin'
it oot, an' A said to him 'Stop!'—*an' he stoppit!* That's the soort o' Mon he is."

My Heart's in the Highlands, Plus Eight Hundred Quid

In which near-millionaire ALAN COREN explains how he owes it all to whisky

OUTWARDLY at least, there is little to connect me with the American grape louse. Whole evenings in my company may be spent without thoughts of this small, yet sturdy, pest crossing the average mind; and, no doubt, those who frequent the environs where this same beastie hangs its hat will testify that my name crops up but rarely in its conversation. If, however, you will bear with me over the next few prosy inches, I promise that this bizarre and intriguing relationship will be explained with all the uncanny precision of a jigsaw puzzle dropping to the floor.

We have to go back to the latter years of the nineteenth century: were I Sir Walter Scott, I should no doubt be able to pinpoint the date as 18—, but that kind of precision died out with unsliced bread and the horse-drawn wireless. If I drop his name here, it is only because we are plunged deep in the strange waters of a Scottish issue, and someone's got to mention the old fool. But it was in the last half of the last century that the American grape louse first raised its ugly head; looked around; and started to eat. By 1900, when it had finished eating, the bottom had dropped out of the brandy market; because what the American grape louse ate, you will be stunned to learn, was grapes. Particularly French grapes. And with the ravaging of the French vineyards, and the consequent punishment undergone by the French booze industry, men hungry for strong spirits dashed away their tears, thought for a moment or two, and turned to whisky. Between 1870 and 1900, whisky production and consumption doubled and redoubled and redoubled again; dozens of new distilleries and companies were built up, and millions of pounds were poured into the business, and millions of gallons were poured down the world's insatiable gullet. Whisky became very big money indeed.

We move on now to April 4, 1964, the next significant date in the history of whisky. It was on that fraught day that my own fate became inextricably linked with that of the unnumerable generations of gorged and dead grape lice; of such arcane fellowships is the story of man on this planet composed.

I had amassed the vast fortune of £794: here is neither space nor time to poke around in the inimical maelstrom of my financial wizardry, to conjure up the procession of grateful heiresses, the international fiscal juggling, the guns for

73

hire, the deep-sea treasure-diving, the diamond smuggling, or the Post Office Savings Account, by which these illimitable riches fell into my hands. We are concerned only with how they fell out of them again. It is a tale to harrow up the blood and make Paul Getty decide to keep the stuff in a trunk under his bed. It is, in short, a story of speculation.

It was at a high-tone soirée upon that fateful April 4 that I chanced to mention the fact of my unparalleled collection of modern British currency; I forget the cause, but believe it had a heaving bust and a predilection for trousers with funds. At all events, my remarks accidentally fell upon the ears of a weasly citizen sniffing nearby, and before I could retract I found myself deep in a conversation about the shakiness of the economy, the paucity of worthwhile investment, the prospect of devaluation, and various other fiduciary topics on which the weasly operator seemed to be a dab hand. It was agreed that capital gains tax had sheared off the fat of stock market investment and property, it was conceded that a bevy of imposts stood poised to lop off profits, rents, fiefs, emoluments and other goodies at the root, and the general drift of the conversation rolled sluggishly towards the conclusion that it was now profitless to invest in anything. Or so I thought: but, as I was about to take my original companion by her upper arm and steer her towards some ill-lit nook, the third party murmured:

"Whisky."

I nodded towards the bar, but he shook his head.

"You ought to invest in whisky," he said.

Intrigued, I paused; and there followed a monologue so weird, so gripping, so complex as to leave the gabby meanderings of the Ancient Mariner at the post. There was, it turned out, a fortune to be made in the Great Whisky Boom, which had boomed on unabated since the heady days of the grape louse feast: millions had been made by men who knew no more about whisky than what you can see from the far end of a siphon. According to my informant (the foam, by this time, flecking his skinny lips), the investor bought single malt whisky in bond, held on to it for a requisite three years while it matured, then flogged it to the distiller who would blend it with two dozen other malts to produce the bottled article; and that three years' tenure produced a profit of two hundred per cent! Moreover, the holding was done elsewhere, in cool Scots warehouses, and the trading was carried out by brokers; the investor did nothing except clear a space in his bank, ready for the imminent lettuce. Amid the drear austerities of 1964, it seemed, I could still clean up.

"But how does one contact a whisky broker?" I cried.

My companion smiled, and blushed.

"You mean . . . ?" I gasped.

He lowered his eyelids modestly. The coincidence was fantastic.

"But, surely," I said, "this is big-time stuff? Surely one needs to invest countless thousands? What is the minimum one can invest?"

"£794," he said,

"No!" I cried.

He nodded.

"By 1967, it will be worth £2,500. Sell and reinvest, and by 1970 it will have shown £7,500."

Integers clacketed in my head.

"By 1980," I exclaimed, "I could be worth a quarter of a million!"

"At a conservative estimate," he said.

Forty years old, an Acapulco tan, the Ferrari murmuring at the gate, my own dinner jacket!

Three days later, it arrived in the post, scroll-worked and invincible-looking: a manuscript to the effect that I owned twenty-five barrels of North of Scotland grain whisky, twelve hundred gallons, lying at Bonhill on the shores of Loch Lomond, working for me. Snapped up at the ridiculously low price of twelve-and-six per gallon. Lovingly, I placed the title-deed in a drawer.

As the drawer closed, the bottom fell out of the whisky market.

Not as I, stricken, suspected; i.e. due to the sudden appearance of the American barley louse, or some such pest, but, according to the financial pages (which I had just begun to read—a little late, perhaps), because of a sudden glut on the market. It had waited a hundred years to glut; and it has glutted on ever since. While the rest of the investing world, in its flight from the pound (not to mention its flight from whisky), started to make strange and unanticipated fortunes out of old silver, postage stamps, cigarette cards, old socks, and God knows what else, my twelve hundred gallons and I stood still for six long years. Worse: it turned out that you can't just leave Scotch in its shed; it has to be coddled, insured, supervised, to the shrill tune of around, in my case fifty quid a year. By 1970, I had forked out a total of £1,100 for booze that refused to make a penny.

So I decided to pay it a visit. That, at least, is one of the things about investing in Scotch: if you've put your money in stocks and shares and insurance and so on, you can't turn up at the doors of Marks and Sparks with a request to see £794 worth of capital, you can't burst in on Cunard and ask to see your bit of *QE2*. But whisky, if nothing else, is *there*; the barrels are numbered, the stuff is palpably *owned*.

You will not find Bonhill on the average map of Scotland: it takes a trained geographer to find it on a map of Bonhill. It lies five miles north of Dumbarton, and is noticeable mainly by its smell: spend an hour in the immediate neighbourhood, and you wake up next morning with hammers in the head, a furry tongue, and eyes like glace cherries. Whisky fills the bright air like invisible smog. I could see the serried ranks of warehouses, spread out down the hill beside the road; I found an opening in the battered fence, and drove in, along the unmade track, beneath the cracked and peeling signs that warned off Unauthorised Visitors. But who was Authorised, if not I?

As I parked outside the hutted office, a man in a pinstripe suit and a man in a Customs and Excise uniform walked over to the car. "I've come to see my whisky," I said. I waved my title deed. They paled a little. Inside me, a stone dropped through the chilled numbles: was it like the Great New Jersey Salad Oil

Infuriated porter. "Ye muckle sumph! Hiv Ah no telt ye twice that the Edinbory Express'll be bizzin' through in hauf a meenit?"
Inebriated Scot. "Man, ye're awfu' feart fur yer Edinbory Express."

Country Gentleman (who thought he'd got such a treasure of a new gardener). "Tut, tut, tut! Bless my soul, Saunders! How——what's all this? Disgracefully intoxicated at this hour of the morning! Ain't you ashamed of yourself?!"
Saunders. "'Sh-hamed! *(Hic.)* Na, na, 'm nae sae drunk as that comes t'! Ah ken varra weel what a'm aboot!!"

Swindle? Was there nothing in my barrels except best Firth of Clyde? Had they been caught out after long years of profitable conning?

"Nobody ever comes to look at their whisky," said the Excise man.

"It's all right," said the main in the suit, and went away.

Minutes passed.

He came back with two short, gnarled men in khaki dungarees. He beckoned me to follow. We walked across the gravel, and into a long, shadowed canyon between the enormous warehouses. Other men in uniforms and overalls appeared at the huge open doors, and stared. One of my dungareed escorts shouted:

"He's come tae see his whusky!"

The message passed from lip to ear along the lines of workers: it was a Bateman cartoon, fleshed and animated. The Sassenach Who Came To See His Whisky. What old Anglo-Scots mistrusts and preconceptions jostled in that encounter! English money invested in the mystical Scotch, the moneyed colonialist arriving suddenly to check on the traditional suspicion of things being put over on him, the Throgmorton Street absentee capitalist and the calloused worker. It was a long walk.

Inside the warehouse, it was cool, and dark, and pungent. A million gallons of Scotch stood barrelled floor to ceiling for what looked like miles on end, the malty silence punctuated only by the plunking drip of condensation. Not speaking, the party led me to a rack, and a ladder, and we all went up it, groping behind a swinging lamp. The lamp was shone along a line of tuns; and there they were. My twenty-five.

"We canna open one, ye ken," said a dungaree.

Behind me, there was a soft snort.

"It's all right," I said. "I just wanted to see it."

"Aye," they said.

We all went out again, in the same silence, under the same long line of eyes. A light touch, I thought, is required.

"If the worst comes to the worst," I said, "can I drink it myself?" The party stopped.

"He wants tae know if he can drink it!" shouted the dungaree.

Someone opened the car door, and I got in.

"We'll not let it oot of our sight," said the pinstriped suit.

I let in the clutch, and bounced back up the broken track. On either side, old cars, de-engined, lay rusting among bent barrels and bethistled piles of planks, sapping any remaining confidence. The scene was like something from *The Grapes Of Wrath*.

If they ever want to make *The Barley Of Wrath,* I reflected, I know where they can get a scriptwriter. He may not be the best, but he's certainly the cheapest. He'll do anything for £794.

Old Scotch Beater (recovering from a collapse, the result of a slight shooting accident). "What's that ye hae been giving me? Whusky? And me unconscious!"

Housekeeper. "Losh me, Laird, ye'll no have asket all thae folks to stop the nicht? There isna beds for the half o' them."
Laird. "Hoots, woman! dinna fash yersel. Gie them plenty whiskey and they'll find beds for themsels."

One for the High Road

HUGH McILVANNEY toasts Scotland's drinkers

THE outsider's impression of Scottish drinking habits is polluted with fallacies. There is, for instance, a relentless inclination to exaggerate the toughness of Glasgow pubs. Experience suggests that the worst of them could be taken by the Red Army in three days, a day-and-a-half if tactical nuclear weapons were used. Of course, the Russians would have to expect an immediate retaliatory strike, a deadly hail of McEwan's screwtops descending on Moscow, a million cairry-oots darkening the sky. The advent of the beer can, with its suspect aerodynamic qualities, may have reduced the standard of long distance throwing among Glaswegians but in an emergency the old skills would reassert themselves. Contrary to what big Alex may think, Brezhnev would get the message.

It would be wrong to give the idea that Glasgow is the only place in Scotland where serious swallowing is done. In sheer volume of the hard stuff consumed, the Highlanders and Islanders yield to no one. Inverness County Council recently found it necessary to send a task-force of refuse collectors from the mainland to North Uist to clear away the cairns of empty whisky bottles that were growing all over the island like the shrines of a pagan cult. However, nearly all the empties were half-bottles, so the Hebrideans had retained a sense of proportion. A sense of proportion is anathema to the Glasgow drinker. When he goes at the bevvy it is a fight to the death.

The attitude is vividly demonstrated when new and allegedly potent drinks are put upon the market. Brewers know what they are doing when they inscribe their labels with warnings. "This beer is especially strong and should not be drunk to excess" is the kind of wording that amounts to an irresistible invitation in Maryhill or Bridgeton. A friend of mine tells me of being present when one of the troops responded to such a challenge. He was found imbibing a much vaunted strong ale called Final Selection along with large shots of Glayva, a liqueur that bears more than a passing resemblance to syrup. My friend was slightly awed by the performance but before he could intervene the field researcher made a pronouncement. "See these," he said. "These is rubbish. Ah've had nine o' them and nine Glayvas and there's no a stagger in me. A waste o' money."

That philosophy is reflected in the raw functionalism of the classic Glasgow drinking emporium. Some of them are so bare that anyone who wants to drink in sophisticated surroundings takes his glass into the lavatory. The maximum decoration in such places is likely to be a photograph of Rangers of Celtic or of Benny Lynch, looking out from under a hair parting that looks as if it was made by a neuro-surgeon. The minders in these establishments are the kind of gentlemen who are reluctant to throw troublemakers out into the street. They prefer to lock the baddies in and have a heart to heart talk.

Naturally, there are times when customer control has to be permitted, when the whims and peccadilloes of the clientele have to be indulged. I remember one such occasion in a pub near Bridgeton Cross after a Celtic-Rangers match. An American magazine had commissioned a photographer and myself to do a piece on that cultural phenomenon and we were walking away from the ground in company with a small Kilmarnock man more noted for his wit than his courage. Our attention was drawn to one particular hostelry because its swing doors were bolted open and inside fourteen or fifteen Rangers supporters were dancing in a circle with their feet crunching on discarded pint glasses. They had linked arms and were singing "Aye, Aye Yippy, the Pope's a f—— hippy."

When the photographer and I decided on a tentative investigation of the scene, I advised the Kilmarnock man to remain on the other side of the street. "Don't worry," he said. "The Man in the Iron Mask wouldnae go in there. Elliot Ness and the Untouchables would be seven-to-four against." His judgement was sound. The cameraman had been on the premises no more than a few seconds when a man with a countenance like an A.A. road map took him by the arm. "Look, son," he said. "Why don't you go away home before you get a terrible sore face." It seemed the wrong time to argue for the rights of the Press, so we strolled away casually about 25 miles an hour.

Some of the belligerence to be encountered is more appealing. A Home Counties rugby player of my acquaintance tells of arriving in Glasgow with two of his mates from the club and finding them in a mood to seek instant refreshment. Having Scottish connections, he sensed the hazards of entering the first pub they came across and counselled patience. The Central Hotel was the place they needed, he suggested. But his arguments were overwhelmed by the thirst of the others and soon they were walking into one of those vast, austere bars that are so common in the suburban areas of the city. It was just after the morning opening hour and the place was almost empty and unnaturally still, like a cathedral with sawdust. One small wizened barman was drifting about behind the counter, with a dish towel over his shoulder, affecting a professional interest in the taps and optics. The breezy entrance of the rugby men did not diminish the sourness of his mood. They started out by asking for bitter which baffled the little man until he discovered that they meant heavy. Then one of the visitors made an appalling error. Holding his glass up into an angled shaft of sunlight, he winced at what he saw and boomed: "This beer's a bit cloudy, isn't it?" The barman sighed wearily. "What do you want for 22p?" he said. "Thunder and lightning?" The chaps went to the Central Hotel.

The English are probably the ultimate authorities on the drinking habits of the

80

"A NARROW ESCAPE"

(Fragment overheard the other day)

"Well, Lauchie, how are you?"

"Man, I'm wonderfu' weel, considerin'."

"Considerin'—what?"

"I did last nicht what I've no dune this thirty year. I gaed to bed *pairfutly sober,* and I'm thankfu' to say I got up this mornin' *no a bit the waur.*"

Host. "Hoots, man! Yer shairly no gangen the noo! The nicht's jest begun."

Guest. "Na, I'm no gangen; but I thocht I wad jest say guid-nicht while I recognise ye!"

Scots. Once every two years, when Scotland play football at Wembley, Londoners in particular are given more opportunities than they need to study the awesome variety of disasters that can be precipitated by a Scotsman's collision with the barley bree. But some Southerners are slow learners. After one international I saw an extremely County couple making their way back to the Rolls with their plaid rugs and their brandy flasks. At the foot of a flight of steps outside the stadium they came upon a living caricature of a Glasgow drunk, the sort of man who, in Billy Connolly's phrase, would have been trying to outstare a chip if he'd had a chip. He was leaning against a wall like a puppet with woodworm. His bonnet was down over his face and his eyelids looked as if each of them weighed a stone.

"Oh John," said the lady. "Look at that poor man. Can't we do something to help him?" John was alert enough to see that the situation might become complicated but his wife was insistent and at last he approached the casualty. "Look, can we help you at all? I mean, could we give you a lift somewhere? The Rolls is just over there. Where would you like us to drop you?"

The drunk slowly contorted his face into an expression of deep concentration. "Very good o' ye," he said at last. "Drop me at Buccleuch Street." Perhaps John did not know that Buccleuch Street was on the south side of Glasgow but he had sufficient nous to make his excuses and leave.

Inevitably, the Wembley invasion gives a distorted picture of the Scottish way of boozing. During that weekend amateurs and part-timers can pass themselves off as the real thing. The only proper place to study the Scottish drinker is in his natural habitat, in all those thousands of pubs where the liquor releases the basic romanticism of the race, where the chat frequently takes on a surrealistic quality. Beef Murphy exemplifies the genre. Beef has enough fantasies to make Walter Mitty look like a boring pragmatist. My favourite concerns the time during his wartime naval service when he was on the bridge of his destroyer with the captain. He must have been in a good mood that day to allow the captain on the bridge with him. Anyway, a U-Boat surfaced about six hundred yards away and Beef, having scanned the enemy through his binoculars, informed his skipper that the German commander was about to torpedo them. "How do you know, Murphy?" asked the captain. "Because," said Beef, "I can lip-read in ten languages."

Beef is also the man who wrote all the James Bond stories and he is not too pleased about the way Ian Fleming stole the manuscripts. He'll tell you about himself some time if you drop in on him at the Goldberry in Kilmarnock. Bring plenty of money. Beef likes a good refreshment. When he can't drink any more beer he throws it up in the air and runs under it.

"Oh goodie! Somebody's been eating my porage."

"Oh please! Your Highness . . . not the Glasgow Empire!"

Chapter Five

For the Sake of Old Long Since: a look at language

The Scots enjoy a great advantage over the English as far as language is concerned. Not only can they pronounce the letter 'r', which the English are unable to, but they have the resources of two languages to draw on—their own and English. Nor is this a matter of history; the other day I read a soccer report in a Scottish newspaper which contained five words entirely new to me, 'blooter', 'stoater', 'juked', 'skited' and 'tanking'. Perhaps I should have known all five, but most Englishmen seem even more ignorant than I am, unaware for instance that 'fou' (or 'fu') means 'drunk' or that a cleg is a kind of horse-fly.

This chapter, then, will be welcomed by all Scots readers as a small monument to the ignorance of the English.

Miss Nan (to new gardener). "Mackay, I wonder if you could possibly use fewer Scotch words when you are talking to my mother? Words like 'neeps' and 'kale runts' and 'tatties', you know."

Mackay. "Dinna fash yersel'. Yer mither's nae a fule, an' gin ye gie her time she'll tummle t'ull't. An' it's nae 'tatties'—it's 'taaaties.'"

Tommy (to Jock, on leave): "What about the lingo? Suppose you want an egg over there, what do you say?"

Jock: "Ye juist say, 'oof."

Tommy: "But suppose you want two?"

Jock: "Ye say 'twa oofs, 'and the silly auld fule wife gies ye three, and ye juist gie her back one. Man, it's an awfu' easy language."

Brush Up Your Lallans

MILES KINGTON

"WEEL," I said, "it's a braw bricht Weltanschauung that blows naebody some guid."

"Agreed," said Cockburn, "but wha ha'd thocht the ould bothy to ha' sae much life in't?"

"Sonsie knaves," blustered Taylor, "dinna ye ken what Nietzsche said?"

"Aye," we both grinned, "the muckle laddie!"

Deep into the night we sat, trying to fan into flames the smouldering embers of the Scottish Lowlands dialect or Lallans, as we connoisseurs knew it to be called. Cockburn suggested pouring petrol over the whole affair, just to see what would happen.

"Wha!" cried Taylor.

"Losh!" I exclaimed.

There was an awkward silence. Neither Taylor nor I was completely convinced that Cockburn took the whole business seriously enough. He had just written the autobiographical notes for the cover of his first novel and it had come as a shock to us to find that they were not in Lallans. We could not help suspecting that he also intended to write the novel in modern English.

"Weel noo," said Taylor, clapping the disconsolate Cockburn on the shoulder, "it's only a wee bittie time to Hogmanay and then ye can recite the whole of Macgregor's Lament for us!"

"By god!" swore Cockburn, "ye'd stab your grandmither for a drop o' the hard stuff, and here ye are havering aboot the likes o' Macgregor!"

"Ma grandmither! And Macgregor! What filthy talk is this? Is it a fecht ye're wanting?"

"Ye watch your lug and I'll watch mine!" shouted Cockburn.

"Och, but it's gae sad to see a guid man go," muttered Taylor, hurling himself ferociously on Cockburn. Quickly I parted them so that we could settle down to a discussion of the foregoing improvisation. Cockburn was of the opinion that he would have held up his end better if he had been inflamed with drink. Taylor took the hint and produced the bottle.

"Aye," said Cockburn, "there's nae water like Spey water and nae cockles like the cockles o' the heart."

"There'll be nae filthy language in ma hoose," said Taylor. "I'm a God-fearin' man, and the same goes for God."

"Awa' and put on your Sunday breeks," scoffed Cockburn.

"Would that I had niver lived tae hear trousers and the Sabbath mentioned in the self-same breath," cried Taylor.

And so crying, he drew an unsuspected dirk and once more leapt upon Cockburn. This time it took rather longer to pull him off; when he was finally sitting in moody silence again, Cockburn and I glanced rather despondently at each other. We were both secretly afraid of Taylor's amazing physical strength—next year he intended to enter for the Highland Fling and we knew that he had already attained considerable distances in practice. I decided to state a calmer theme for our variations.

"Weel, 'tis a bonnie nicht and nae mistake."

"Bonnie is as bonnie does," grumbled Taylor. "A' is vanity, as it says in the Good Book."

"Ye mean the Guid Buik?" said Cockburn quickly.

"Ah ken fine what Ah mean," shouted Taylor, "and I'll thank ye no' to poke your nose in where's nae smell!"

"Now I ca' on God as my witness," said Cockburn, "that there was nae malice nor guile in what I said, and as God is no' here in tangible form, I ca' on our guid friend here to back me up."

The both turned to me expectantly. I thought rapidly and opened my mouth.

"Wheesht," I said.

"Look, I'm sorry," I said, "can we do that bit again? I won't let you down this time."

"Oh, what's the point," said Cockburn. "Taylor and I have been doing all the work while you've been sitting there just like an apprehensive hedgehog."

"Recent experiments show," I said, "that far from being apprehensive, the hedgehog will display amazing ferocity when its amour-propre has been wounded."

"Recent experiments show," said Taylor, "that you have no idea how to pronounce amour-propre."

"Trust Taylor to know all about these new-fangled French diseases," jeered Cockburn.

The ensuing free improvisation in modern English lasted for half an hour and was full of happy verbal invention. Unfortunately Cockburn, Taylor and I have not spoken to each other since that day, so the Lallans revival movement may be said to have completely expired, but at least we have carried on the good old Scottish Lowlands tradition by replacing it with a deadly three-sided family feud.

News that rich Arabs are buying up Scottish land and castles and moving in could not have come at a better time for Scottish poetry . . .

TO A CAMEL

Gret, reekin, moldie, mangie beastie,
O, welcome tae oor humble feastie!
Who wad hae thought ye quite so tastie,
        Wi' neeps and tatties?
Come, set we doon and gobble hastie
        Oor camel patties!

SHAIKH LOCH-IN-VAR

O, Shaikh Loch-in-Var is come out of the
   East,
Through all the wide Border, his steeds
   are the best!
A puce Lamborghini, a carmine Ferrari,
   plus two yellow Rollses, drives
   Shaikh Loch-in-Var!

He roars through the Highlands at over
   the ton,
Pursued in her Alfa by Wife Number One,
Who's followed by Wives Two, Three, Four,
   in *their* cars!
Was there ever a harem like
   Shaikh Loch-in-Var's?

Behind speeds their eunuch (who really
   quite likes
The sensation you get on the big motor bikes!)
His thighs grip the flanks of his white Yamaha,
As he screams in the wake of young
   Shaikh Loch-in-Var!

As they watch him whizz past, the pedestrian
   Scots
Dream their own dreams of concubines,
   Bentleys, and yachts;
And they shout at the flash of his bright
   djellibah:
"Just ye wait till we've got our *own* oil,
   Loch-in-Var!"

       ★

TO A SHEEP'S EYE

Fair fa' your honest sonsie face,
Great chieftain o' the organ race!
Aboon them a' ye tak your place,
   Ears, nose, and throat!
Weel are ye worthy o' a grace
   As lang's my coat!

SHAIKHS, WHA HAE

Shaikhs, wha'hae wi' Faisal bled,
Shaikhs Yamani's aften led,
Welcome tae your oily bed,
   Or tae victorie!

Noo's the day, and noo's the hour!
Charge you BP drilling-tower!
Sod the Minister o' Power!
   Hoots monopolie!

       ★

THE TWA CORBIES

As I was walking all alane,
I heard twa corbies[1] making a mane:
The tan unto the tither did say,
"Where sall we gang and sell this day?"

"In behint you auld fail[2] brake
I wot there sits an oil-rich shaikh;
And naebody kens that he lies there
But his wazir, his goat, and his ladies fayre."

"Why!" quoth tither, "Here's luck, the noo!
We'll sell him a brool[3] and a fustie[4], too!
A diggle[5] and aye a comlie crake[6]!
He'll nae ken the difference, you wogglie
   shaikh!"

---

[1]Corbies=estate agents   [2]fail=turf   [3]brool=derelict farmland
[4]fustie=fake castle [5]diggle=mountain
[6]crake=island with no planning permission

The Lunnon Twang

I've heard a Frenchman wag his tongue
   Wi' unco din an' rattle,
An', 'faith, my vera lugs hae sung
   Wi' listenin' tae his prattle;
But French is no the worst of a'
   In point o' noise an' clang, man;
There's ane that beats it far awa',
   And that's the Lunnon twang, man.

You wadna think, within this land,
   That folk could talk sae queerly,
But, sure as death, tae understand
   The callants beats me fairly.
An', 'faith, 'tis little gude their schules
   Can teach them, as ye'll see, man,
For—wad ye credit it?—the fules
   Can scarcely follow *me,* man.

An' yet, tae gie the deils their due,
   (An' little praise they're worth, man,)
They seem tae ken, I kenna hoo,
   That I come frae the Nor-r-th, man!
They maun be clever, for ye ken
   There's nought tae tell the chiels, man:
I'm jist like a' the ither men
   That hail frae Galashiels, man.

But oh! I'm fain tae see again
   The bonny hills an' heather!
Twa days, and ne'er a drap o' rain—
   Sic awfu, drouthy weather!
But eh! I doubt the Gala boys
   Will laugh when hame I gang, man,
For oo! I'm awfu' feared my voice
   Has ta'en the Lunnon twang, man!

And Ne'er Made Sic Anither!

ALEX ATKINSON

An emotional outburst, in the friendliest possible manner, on the delicate subject of Robert Burns, born January 25, 1759

MANY a time on Burns Night, when I am merry with drink[1] and the hoar-frost[2] glitters on the sill, I am moved to marvel at the power the Ayrshire poet has to stir, uplift and influence me, a Sassenach. For true it is that ever since I was a child[3] his mystic lines have haunted my daydreams, colouring the drab spaces of my imagination, and giving force and depth even to my most casual conversation.

I have frequently called out, for example, in the midst of some smart[4] cocktail-party, seeing a friend make off through the fug for the door,

> *"Ha! whare ye gaun, ye crowlin ferlie!"*

and a hush has fallen over the scene of elegant debauch: English men and women all, they have paused in their sipping, arrested by the magic of a line which they have never fully understood, yet which has stayed in their unconscious minds since first they lisped its syllables from some forbidden book. (What it actually means is "Hey! Where are *you* off to? You're fairly stinking.")

Again, I have been pleased at times[5], in some sleek[6] restaurant where ladies of fashion peck their way through bird or troutlet, to order a daimen-icker and watch the waiter search his memory. "And bring it in a thrave, if you please," I have requested.

> *A daimen-icker in a thrave*
> *'S a sma request,*

or so one would think: but no waiter has yet succeeded in bringing me one, sizzling in its rich gravy, the silver-plated thrave swaddled in a costly napkin, with apple-pie and custard to follow. I see this icker (the *daimen*-icker is the large size, with the head left on the bone: it would be sufficient for two persons, and is rather ostentatious) as a kind of baby dragon, cooked slowly in whisky and browned under the grill just before serving.

When at last the penny drops for the waiter, and he makes the age-old response,

---

1 fou   2 cranreuch   3 wean   4 braw   5 whyles   6 sleekit

> *"I'll get a blessin' wi' the lave,*
> *And never miss't"*

(meaning exactly what it says), he smiles at me, as at an old friend. It is at such moments that we realise there is a little Scotch in all of us.

But it is to our romantic side that Burns' potent strains do chiefly speak.

> *My plaidie to the angry airt,*
> *I'd shelter thee, I'd shelter theee . . .*

Which one among[1] us can fail to respond to the poignancy of the picture here presented, of the simple ploughman kneeling down to shelter his beloved plaidie, while the airts move up angrily on every side? To the best of my knowledge I have yet to come across an airt, and I have but a muddy[2] notion of a plaidie; yet such lines as these beat in my head[3] like the wild notes of a rustic pipe, bringing strange scenes before my inward eye. They have a universal ring, and it is not hard to see how they have entranced even the inhabitants of the U.S.S.R., who are known to be pretty[4] choosey.

> *Duncan fleech'd, and Duncan pray'd:*
> *May was deaf as Ailsa Craig . . .*

Here is this Duncan—I don't know how Khrushchev sees him, but I see him as a red-bearded, thickset youngster with his bonnet awry[5], like a bear with a sore[6] head—here he is fleeching all over the flagstoned cottage in the most abandoned way, pausing now and then to pray, or knock his pipe out. And here is this poor May, as deaf as an onion, unable to tell for certain whether he is fleechin' or lowpin', and too proud[7] to tell him to go[8]. It is the sort of scene that might be enacted on any Saturday night, say around ten-thirty, from Culloden to Lima.

I should perhaps[9] admit here that Burns' lines have not stayed in my head in any kind of proper order. Few Englishmen would be bold enough to claim this, I think. There are odd, majestic snatches only, full of a wondrous meaning but dreamily mingled, forming at last a mosaic of images, wise saws and striking tableaux. Sometimes, feeling unusually blithe and gay[10], I will carol out a stanza, letting it fall where it will

> *"And naething, now, to big a new ane—*
> *Grat his een baith bleer't and blin.*
> *O wad ye tak a thought an' men',*
> *My bonie lady!*
> *Drumossie moor—Drumossie day—*
> *The best-laid schemes o' Mice an' Men,*
> *I'm wae to think upo' you den:*
> *All mimsy were the borogroves*
> *O' foggage green!"*

---

1 amang   2 drumlie   3 pow   4 unco   5 a-gley   6 sair   7 skeigh   8 gang   9 aibline   10 crouse and canty

No man who has ever grat his een over a bony lady, stumbling through the foggage of Drumossie moor, could fail to be moved by this, I think, however vague may be his interpretation of any particular phrase in it: and this is the measure of the mysterious power of Burns—a power unequalled in the whole field of lyric poetry with the possible exception of a page or two of Ezra Pound. Lang then may his lum reek, is my humble wish. Lang may he continue to befeazle me with phlu and lawpie, grooting his dil aboon and aside[1] to the delight of hulp and magger. In fact, dear Bob, if I may thus address you,

>...*mishanter fa' me*
>*If thoughts o' thee, or yet thy mamie,*
>*Shall ever daunton me or awe me*...

And so good night[2].

---

1 abeigh   2 guid nicht

THE RETURN OF THE NATIVE
Tam. "Sae ye've gotten back, Sanders?"
Sanders. "'Deed, aye. I've just gotten back."
Jamie. "An' hoo did 'e like London?"
Sanders. "Od, it's an ootlandish place yon! They tell't me they couldna unnerstaun ma awccent!"
John. "Awccent! I never heard tell that Fife folk had *ony* awccent!"

Rigs Awa'

FROM THE LAYS OF A LAZY MINSTREL

Haggis broo is bla' and braw,
Kittle kail is a' awa';
Gin a lassie kens fu' weel,
Ilka pawkie rattlin' reel.
    Hey the laddie! Oh the pladdie!
    Hey the sonsie Finnie haddie!
        Hoot awa'!

Gang awa' wi' philibegs,
Maut's nae missed frae tappit kegs;
Sound the spleuchan o' the stanes,
Post the pibrock i' the lanes!
    Hey the swankie, scrievin' shaver!
    Ho the canny clishmaclaver!
        Hoot awa'!

Paritch glowry i' the ee,
Mutchkin for a wee drappee;
Feckfu' is the barley-bree—
Unco' gude! Ah! wae is me!
    Hey the tousie Tullochgorum!
    Ho the mixtie-maxtie jorum!
        Hoot awa'!

The Twenty-fifth

W. C. DUNCAN

[Note.—For the benefit of poor illiterate Sassenachs it should perhaps be explained that the 25th of January is the anniversary of the birth of Scotland's Patron Saint, Robert Burns. The occasion is celebrated by Scotsmen the world over with loyal and solemn ceremony.]

Scene: A City Street

Two men who have just met are shaking hands cordially. It is obvious from a casual glance at them that they have some sentiment in common.

FIRST MAN. Hullo, old chap! Feeling fit? Tonight's the night, you know.

SECOND MAN. Fit as a fiddle and looking forward to the haggis and what not immensely.

[All at once they pause and a thought seems to strike them simultaneously.]

FIRST MAN *(coughing slightly)*. Weel, ma cantie callant, I'm pleased tae hae met ye again. Ye maun hae a drap o' the auld Kirk wi' me.

SECOND MAN *(nervously)*. Thanks, I————Man, it's unco guid o' ye, and I'll no say naw.

[They enter arm-in-arm a nearby bar.]

FIRST MAN *(to waitress)*. Here, lassie, see's twa glesses o' yule.

[He is rather proud about this and glances slyly at his friend to see how he is taking it.]

SECOND MAN *(triumphantly)*. And dinna be blate aboot it.

[The waitress, guessing correctly, brings the whisky and is not a little surprised at receiving prompt payment. Indeed she tests the coins unobtrusively with her teeth.]

BOTH MEN *(together)*. Weel, here's tae us.

[There is a pause while they both recover their breaths.]

FIRST M . And hoo's the guidwife and the wee bits o' bairns?

SECOND MAN. Brawly, thenk ye; they're a' daein' fine.

[Both, as can be seen from their anxious expressions, are beginning to feel the strain.]

95

SECOND MAN (*suddenly*). Aiblins ye'll tak anither wee drappie?

[*The* FIRST MAN *nods without speaking, for he is mentally noting that word "aiblins" for future use. The* SECOND MAN *feels that he has scored heavily. They drink again in silence, each not being too sure of the proper words to say this time.*]

FIRST MAN (*proudly and loudly*)—
> For a' that an' a' that,
> It's comin yet for a' that,
> That man to man the world o'er
> Shall man to man the world o'er
> Shall brithers be for a' that.

SECOND MAN (*not to be outdone*)—
> Wee, sleekit, cowrin, tim'rous beestie,
> O, what a panic's in they breastie!
> Thou need na start awa—

[*He stops there, having forgotten the rest. The other people
in the bar are beginning to look at him.*]

SECOND MAN (*nervously*). Pretty warm in here—er————Mind ye, it's unco het in here. I'm fair ramfeezled wi' it.

FIRST MAN. That's so, I think I'll toddle—that is, I'll hae taw gang awa' the noo.

SECOND MAN. Ay. It's gey late.

[*They leave the bar slowly, trying to think of other Scots words
to use until they reach the street again.*]

FIRST MAN. Weel, we'll be seeing ye the nicht (*moves off*).

[*The* SECOND MAN *merely waves his hand and retires in the opposite direction. All at once he turns round and runs after his friend, but cannot find him. Which is a pity, because had just remembered two good words, "tapsalteerie" and "forjeskit".*]

"Aiblins"

Sweet "Aiblins," word of plaintive cheer,
What wealth, what wonderment is here!
   No sound of early Spring
Is half so searching or so deep;
I have been often moved to weep
   Since first I heard the thing.

It came to me beyond the Forth:
Some scraggy wilding of the North
   Answered me thus one day.
At first I felt but little change,
Saving that something rich and strange
   Had shone upon my way.

But by degrees, as on I drew,
Its rapture warmed me through and through
   For all my daylong tramp,
Till dale and loch and mountain rang
With "Aiblins" as I sang and sang,
   Although my feet were damp.

I know not why I love, nor whence
Derives its blessed influence;
   Its meaning, too, who knows?
The simple charm suffices me;
Who would dissect a melody?
   Who scrutinise the rose?

Should any delve it to the roots,
No doubt 'tis kin to "havers," "hoots,"
   And all the rich surprise
Of mystic sounds that Scotsmen make
Which keep the Southron mind awake
   In passionate surmise.

I know not these: I only feel
That, if I met a man of steel
   Who did not own its charm
Or scorned its rare and fragrant grace,
I'd try to smack his silly face
   And do him grievous harm.

Oh, tell it o'er in gentle tone;
Would it not melt a heart of stone
   And make the dourest glad?
We cannot show its like (more shame)
Save "chilblains," which is not the same,
   But cold, and dull and sad.

For me it has a lasting spell
Of comfort, even when I'm well;
   And, when my strength is plucked
From off me and my last hour nears,
Then breathe it in my failing ears
   And I shall feel quite bucked.

Dum-Dum

ISOLATION!—OFF THE ORKNEYS

Southern Tourist. "Get any newspapers here?"
Orcadian Boatman. "Ou aye, when the steamer comes. If it's
fine, she'll come ance a week; but when it's stormy, i' winter,
we dinna catch a glint o' her for three months at a time."
S.T. "Then you'll not know what's goin' on in London!"
O.B. "Na—but ye see ye're just as ill aff i' London as we
are, for ye dinna ken what's gaun on here!"

Sandy (at Victoria Station). "Give me *The Peebles Herald.*"
Attendant. "We don't keep it."
Sandy. "Then just gie me one o' yer local papers."

"We had the shadow of the Bomb, but you have to bear in mind that
they've grown up under the shadow of the Bay City Rollers."

"VITA FUMUS"

Tonal. "Whar'll ye hae been till, Tugal?"
Tugal. "At ta McTavishes' funeral——"
Tonal. "An' is ta Tavish deed?"
Tugal. "Deed is he!!"
Tonal. "Losh, mon! Fowk are aye deein' noo that never used to dee afore!!"

Southerner (in Glasgow, to Friend). "By the way, do you know McScrew?"
Northerner. "Ken McScrew? Oo' fine! A graund man, McScrew! Keeps the Sawbath,—an' everything else he can lay his hands on!"

Chapter Six

A Few Classics

The captions to some Punch cartoons have passed into general usage, and here are eight which most readers will be surprised to learn started life in Punch drawings. Oddly, there is little Scottish about most of them except the accent.

Occasionally jokes have gone down so well that they have been done again in Punch by completely different artists, though quite unwittingly. If anyone from Punch ever tries to tell you that jokes are never repeated, show him the pair of duplicated cartoons included at the end of the section.

"Will ye tak' the paper?"
"Thanks. I don't care for reading in the train."
"Maybe. But will ye kindly cover yer knees wi't? A've nae wish to contemplate them."

Neighbour. "And how's yer guid man this mornin', Mrs. Tamson?"
Mrs. Tamson. "He deed last nicht."
Neighbour. "I'm real sorry to hear that. Ye'll no remember if he happened to say anything about a pot o' green paint before he slippet awa?"

THRIFT

Peebles Body (to townsman who was supposed to be in London on a visit). "E—eh Mac! ye're sune hame again!" *Mac.* "E—eh, it's just a ruinous place, that! Mun, a had na' been the-erre abune twa hoours when—*bang*—went saxpence!!!"

"THE BILLS OF MORTALITY"

Kirk Elder (after a look at his morning paper). "Poor McStagger deid! Et's vera sad to thenk o' the great number o' destengweshed men that's lately been ta'en! 'Deed—I no feel vera weel—mysel'"

CATECHISM UNDER DIFFICULTIES

Free Kirk Elder (preparatory to presenting a tract). "My friend, do you know the chief end of man?" *Piper (innocently).* "Na, I dinna mind the chune! Can ye no whustle it?"!!

Elder MacTavish. "Weel, Donald, an' hoo's the world treating you?" *Donald.* "Verra seldom, Mr. MacTavish."

CANDID

Sportsman. "Boy, you've been at this whiskey!"
Boy (who has brought the luncheon-basket). "Na! The cooark wadna come oot!"

Host. "Hullo! Somone's been at the whisky."
Gillie. "Ah'll tak' ma oath it wasna me. The corrk wadna come oot."

Lady (to new housemaid engaged by letter). "Why didn't you tell me, when you wrote answering my questions so fully, that you were Scotch, Mary?"
Mary. "I didna like to be boasting, Mem."

Chapter Seven

The Tartan Path to Devolution: a look at politics

The *real* Macbeth, it is said, was not the bloody tyrant that Shakespeare depicted but a stable and long-lived ruler who was very reasonable for his age. Another example of the English getting Scottish history all wrong. On the whole, though, Scottish politics have always been a bit of a mess, with as much internal wrangling going on as could be fitted in between forays against the English. It has only been since the Act of Union in 1707 that the Scots have been able to lay the full blame for their misfortunes on the English and nowadays, with the advent of oil, there has been mounted a fairly successful campaign to make the English feel guilty about Culloden, the clearances, George IV looking ridiculous in a kilt, Clydeside ship-building, the theft of footballers by Manchester United and the price of whisky.

How far the current surge towards devolution will go remains to be seen, but one thing seems sure: if it does not work out, the English will be to blame.

MY HALO'S IN THE HIGHLANDS

John Ogilvie having become the first Scot to be canonised, many people must be wondering about all those who have hitherto failed to make it. We have selected three of the most poignant claimants

The Blessed Jimmy o' the Terraces

Fierce controversy continues to rage over the bid for canonisation of the Blessed Jimmy, a diminutive Celtic supporter stomped to pieces by Protestants after the Rangers-Celtic match of 1953. Although his was an authentic martyrdom (fragments of him were found as far north as Lerwick), some doubt remains as to the validity of his miracles and the reliability of the witnesses to them: for example, while the Vatican accepts that on three separate occasions the Blessed Jimmy was able to drink eight bottles of Haig and walk unharmed through a plate-glass window, it feels that this may not redound entirely to the credit of the Church; and while it appreciates the boon to Catholics of the glowing toilet-roll which the spirit of the Blessed Jimmy causes to hover over the Celtic goal and mesmerise Protestant strikers, it has been unable to trace a witness who saw the phenomenon while sober. Similarly, no one has been able to corroborate the legend that the nose of the martyr, which stands in a jam jar on the mantelpiece at 43a McNaughton Crescent, Glasgow, begins to run just before home matches, since its owner is one of the Protestants who originally removed it and, when approached by Catholics with a request to view, attacks them with a coke-hammer.

Holy McMoone o' the Loch

On February 15, 1923, Hamish McMoone, a manufacturer of souvenir miniature bagpipes from Kilmarnock, became the first man to see the Loch Ness Monster, and, on February 16, the first man to begin selling miniature Loch Ness Monsters to visiting tourists. How he happened to have a warehouseful of small plaster dinosaurs which, when their heads were turned, played *The Bluebells Of Scotland*, is only one of the many miracles manifested by the Holy McMoone. However, by 1933, the area was so swamped by other souvenir establishments that McMoone found it impossible to continue in business. Three days after going bankrupt, he was seen by his wife to be walking across the surface of Loch Ness; then, as she watched, the waters opened, and the Monster put its head out and ate him. The national press coverage was such that Mrs McMoone not only managed to put her business back on an even keel, she also opened The Monster Hotel next door and, early in 1934, The Monster Miniature Railway And Lido. The business flourished, and, in 1939, she married Duncan Corkwurral of Aberdeen. For thirty years, the Corkwurrals made a very good living from the establishment, but the current economic climate has brought leaner times. Last year, Mrs Corkwurral applied to the Vatican to have her late husband canonised, offering the Church twenty-five per cent of the profits on plaster busts of the saint, Miracle McMoone Shortbread, and bottles of Loch Ness Miracle Sciatica Cure Water. The deal had all but gone through when Duncan Corkwurral went into hospital for an emergency tonsillectomy, for which, while he was under the angesthetic, his beard was shaved, revealing the face of Hamish McMoone. Although Mrs McMoone is claiming that this is still further evidence of the miraculous powers of her late husband in being able to resurrect himself at will, the Vatican has suspended work on the contract until further proof is offered, or until their percentage is increased to fifty per cent.

The Wee Martyr o' Nigg

It now seems unlikely that the Pope will intervene personally in the case of Archibald McPhoon, the Wee Martyr o' Nigg, who was shovelled to death when oil was discovered on him in April 1973. "Issa justa lousy luck," was how the Cardinal in charge of the Beatification Enquiry put it in his letter to McPhoon's Bishop. The facts are these: during the early months of 1973, oil fever in the north of Scotland had reached so frenzied a pitch that everything from motorways to golf courses were being ruthlessly dug up in the hope of finding on-shore oil deposits. Nigg, centre of the rig industry, was a prime target for oil-seeking carpetbaggers, since it was not only believed to stand above the North Sea Oil Lake, it also contained all the technological wherewithal to extract the stuff should it be found. At 11.46 on the morning of April 9, Archibald McPhoon slid out from beneath the family Cortina which he had been servicing, stood up, and was beginning to wipe the oil from his face and arms when he was pounced on by a mob of some thirty prospectors who, within seconds, had dug him to nothing. It is said that every Bank Holiday, Archibald McPhoon returns and fouls the beach, but, in the opinion of Rome, this is not a major enough manifestation for what the Cardinal concerned has called "the bigga one."

Scottish Nationalism is an English Problem

JIMMY REID

'We've drunk to our English brother (But he does not understand)"
—Rudyard Kipling

SOME years ago I was attending an international conference of young trade unionists. At the hotel you had to fill in a card of nationality. I put *Scottish*. An observant English friend said, "You bloody nationalist." His form stated *Nationality: English*.

The national problem in Britain is in England. The exaggerated claims and enthusiams of the Scots on such occasions as the biennial pilgrimage to Wembley are a cry for recognition—"Look at us," they are saying; "we are Scots! Call us British and we won't demur, but after that and sometimes even before it we are Scots."

Looked at in the context of Scottish history, before and after the Treaty of Union, this is an understandable attitude. Most English people do not understand—they don't even try. Theirs is the certitude, the unshakable complacent conviction, that Britain is really England. That Scotland is a county just a little bit further north than Lancs. How ungrateful the Scots are, clinging to their Scottishness; they have been more or less invited to join the club. You too can be an Englishman, then like us you won't have to proclaim your national virtues, for they will be so obvious as to need no proclamation.

My square-bashing period covered the festive season. Sent home for Christmas, we had to be back on the 28th December. I protested; the RAF was British, not English, so the service should respect Scottish traditions as well. Our main festivity was at the New Year.

"Bloody heathens," said the NCO.

I pointed out that a midwinter festival predated Christianity, and anyway *was* Christ born on the 25th December? Had *he* seen the birth certificate? In my opinion He was born on the 1st January.

All to no avail. On 31st December, 1953, in the NAAFI at RAF Bridgnorth, the Scots gathered. As usual there were no spirits on sale. Everything was as usual. For the Scots this was unusual. This was Hogmanay, and they didn't understand. Back in the billet, six of us, all Scots, huddled round the fire. The lights were out, so we waited miserably for the "bells" although there would be no Bells for us, neither chimes nor whisky.

The nub of the matter is quite simple. A proud, independent, small, historically unconquered nation was pushed by its aristocracy into a union with a bigger neighbouring nation that had hitherto been the main threat to its existence. A situation calling for great delicacy. The tendency in such relationships is for the larger nation to swamp by sheer volume and force of numbers the cultural sense of identity and ethnic character of the smaller. This tendency is invariably resisted and defeated. Such is the lesson of history. The English ruling class, anglicised sections of the Scottish nobility, displayed no delicacy; the union, legally between equals, became a cultural and political annexation.

The attitude of English ruling circles was expressed by Henry VII when he offered his daughter Margaret in marriage to James of Scotland. James accepted in the hope that it would consolidate the truce with England. Some of Henry's privy councillors opposed the marriage on the grounds that England might by royal descent fall into the hands of the Scottish crown. His reply was profoundly prophetic: "Supposing, which God forbid, that all my male progeny should become extinct, and the kingdom devolve by law to Margaret's heirs, will England be damaged thereby? For since it ever happens that the less becomes subservient to the greater, the accession will be that of Scotland to England, just as formerly happened to Normandy, which devolved on our ancestors in the same manner, and was happily added to our kingdom by hereditary right, as a rivulet to a fountain."

The Gaelic was banned. Butcher Cumberland sought to destroy the clans. English practice in agriculture and animal husbandry were imported into and grafted onto the Scottish traditions; some were beneficial, others socially and culturally destructive. The other language of Scotland, the Lallans or Erse, was treated contemptuously. Robert Burns was advised to abandon it and write his verse in English if he wanted recognition.

Some people argue too that after the Union Scotland's gross national product increased enormously, and that therefore it was advantageous. They forget that the period after the Union is mainly characterised in the economic field by the Industrial Revolution. By what logic can it be argued that Scotland would have been excluded from this process except for the Union? James Watt, at Glasgow University, invented the rotary engine, and one could catalogue a list of Scots who made outstanding contributions in engineering, textiles and many other fields of technology during the eighteenth and nineteenth centuries. In addition, mineral wealth, rivers, coastal towns and a traditional pattern of trade combined to create favourable possibilities for Scotland. What may be true is that Scotland's laws and customs, left to develop, may have made the Industrial Revolution less painful and harrowing for our people. We will never know for certain.

What we *do* know is that the governmental structure that has evolved since 1707 does not recognise the existence of Scotland as a nation. This was intended. The treaty declares that henceforth there will be no Scotland or England but Britain. Yet nations cannot be erased by bureaucratic decrees, nor military force—Hitler, if he was capable of rational thought, must have realised this, working in his Berlin bunker. The Americans discovered this in South East Asia. More than 250 years after it had been decreed non-existent, Scotland is still a nation, alive and kicking, demanding recognition. It cannot be denied.

As a nation we have a right to self-determination. However, to disentangle the economic and political ties of more than two centuries is well-nigh impossible and not desirable for the Scots or English people. This is a viewpoint of the great majority of Scots. They may well be driven into another position by politicians who continue not to understand. Scottish, English and Welsh assemblies should be established—instead of discussing what should be devolved downwards, we should be considering what powers to invest in the British parliament. This would rectify the injustices of the original treaty and would provide the principal basis for proper relations between the component nations of the UK.

My last point is this. Nationalism and internationalism are indivisible; those who proclaim "I am an internationalist, not a nationalist," are talking nonsense. This is like saying, "I believe water exists, but I accept H_2 and reject O". *Inter* means between; *national* implies a consciousness of nationhood. Some people wrongly associate nationalism with the jingoism of war and the super-race theories of fascism, but this is *chauvinism*. A love of all that's good in one's own people and nation is a necessity to appreciate similar feelings in the hearts and minds of other peoples.

A Welsh poet said to his fellow countrymen, "If you don't love Wales, you can't love the world." I love Scotland. My Scottish heritage is an integral part of my being. I toast my English brother and sister; you belong to the nation that produced Chaucer, Milton, Shakespeare, Keats, Shelley, Sir Francis Bacon, Wat Tyler and the Tolpuddle Martyrs; they belong to England and through England to the world. I respect your pride in being English; please recognise my right to be proud of being a Scot. Such principled and mutual recognition of our national differences is the basis for unity, as citizens of the British Isles.

LIFE IN SCOTLAND

Vandals set fire to drums of anti-vandal chemicals in a storage shed at Bilsland Drive, Glasgow, yesterday. *(Scottish Express)*

It was then that Councillor Little launched his attack. "I move no action," he said, "it is a complete waste of valuable time and money and I think it is incompetent. It is a lot of nonsense that we should even consider discussing it any further. I will bring this matter up later." *(Troon & Prestwick Times)*

MACBETH or LOCAL THANE MAKES GOOD

Through the medium of the Classic Comics (Ivanhoe, Oliver Twist, etc., in full colour, 15 cents each) America leads the world in the presentation of the masterpieces of literature in a brisk and palatable form. We feel it our duty to rally to the support of those of our contemporaries over here who are striving so gallantly to make up Britain's leeway in this important field, and now proudly present our first Classic Comic:—

Look out for more of this on the next page

MACBETH (continued)

113

Act of Disunion

ELIZABETH THE SECOND (and First of Scotland), to her Parliament in Westminster and also to the Parliament in Glasgow, or perhaps Edinburgh, unless the Scots have decided to place it somewhere entirely different for the sake of peace, **GREETINGS!** and **HI THERE, JIMMY!**

WHEREAS it has now been decided that although the Act of Union of 1707 did join the kingdoms of Scotland and England together "for ever after", this should now be taken to mean "or until such time as the people of Scotland can put up with Westminster no longer"; therefore we now declare that the Union of Scotland and England is at an end (the problem of England and Wales being settled separately by the *Act of Rugby Union and Welsh Supremacy*) and that the disunion shall take place according to the following articles:

ARTICLE ONE
THAT no English cartoonist shall depict any Scottish person whatsoever wearing a kilt, sporran, tam-o'-shanter or bagpipes, tossing a caber, dancing a reel or eating porage, without due authorisation from the Scottish Parliament at Stirling, Cumbernauld, Crieff or whatever compromise site shall be agreed on;

ARTICLE TWO
THAT Billy Connolly be referred to in future as the Scottish gross national product;

ARTICLE THREE
THAT the import quota of Scottish footballers, thereby to revivify the English national sport, be restricted to 10,000 strikers, 5,000 midfield players and 3,000 sweepers per year, and that furthermore no Scottish goalkeepers be permitted entry notwithstanding the fact that English football need no further goalkeepers, it being a fact that desperate defence is the only area in which the English do shine;

ARTICLE FOUR
THAT any English person accosting a Scottish national in the street or any other place used for alcoholic refreshment and greeting him with such expressions as "Hoots mon", "Och aye the noo", "Up your kilt", "Ah ken fine" or "Lang may your lum reek", shall be guilty of an offence against the Race Relations Act (English-style);

ARTICLE FIVE
THAT the Calcutta Cup be renamed the Wooden Spoon;

ARTICLE SIX
THAT with the end of the hitherto accepted honours system, certain famous persons shall henceforth be referred to as Mr Walter Scott, Mr Harry Lauder, Mrs Flora Robson, Mary Ms of Scots, etc;

ARTICLE SEVEN
THAT the Scottish Women's Liberation Front be permitted to refer to their enemies as "male Calvinist pigs";

ARTICLE EIGHT
THAT Lord Home be given a free transfer to England in exchange for Willie Hamilton ex-M.P.;

ARTICLE NINE
THAT the Queen's Christmas Broadcast be repeated on SBC-TV as the Queen's Hogmanay Broacast;

ARTICLE TEN
THAT the M8 motorway between Edinburgh and Glasgow be renamed the Mc8;

ARTICLE ELEVEN
THAT such old-fashioned jokes as renaming the Glasgow-Edinburgh road the Mc8 be punishable by a broken bottle in the face or worse;

ARTICLE TWELVE
Aaaaaaaaaargh! Uuuuuuuurf! Glug;

ARTICLE THIRTEEN
THAT if, fed by unbelievable oil revenues, the new Scottish Parliament should become rich beyond the dreams of human avarice or at least of the Economist Intelligence Unit, then the English Parliament should have the option to reconsider its decision to jettison the Act of Union and get its hands on its fair share of the North Sea bonanza;

ARTICLE FOURTEEN
THAT if the Scots make as much of a mess of their independent economy as even their worst friends (= Tory Central Office) feared, then England will stick up for them as they have stuck up for, for instance, their kith and kin in Rhodesia, the pound sterling, Jeremy Thorpe, Princess Margaret and Duncan McKenzie; i.e. doing nothing;

ARTICLE FIFTEEN
FINALLY, that after this unparalleled, epoch-making, earth-shattering severance of powers between our two nations, things shall go on much as before;

ARTICLE SIXTEEN
THAT, let's face it, Celtic and Rangers are rubbish these days;

ARTICLE SEVENTEEN
AND the same, to be royally frank, goes for any English team you care to mention;

ARTICLE EIGHTEEN
SO (and this is what this Act is *really* all about) why don't we get together and pick an all-British team that could wipe the floor with any foreign side invented?

ARTICLE NINETEEN
OH, come *on*!! Kenny Dalgiesh is rubbish and you know it!

ARTICLE TWENTY
RIGHT. If that's your attitude, I'm all for disunion.

—**Elizabeth II** (or I, as the case may be)

RANGERS BOOT BOYS RULE OK

MAN. UNITED —WHA'S LIKE US?

114

My First Year in Office

—A TV Broadcast by the President of Scotland
full text provided by GORDON WILLIAMS

HAVING invented radar, penicillin, the Bank of England, chloroform, steam-power, Sean Connery, electric soup and the Paisley pattern, it is my firm conviction that we inventive, industrious, eminently logical Scots can make a success of our new independent nation and I would say, on this first anniversary of Home Rule, that all we have to fear is McPhee himself.

I refer, of course, to ex-Bailie Vladimir McPhee, whose grandiose personal ambitions have led to this current tension with the self-styled Independent People's Republic of Fife. As first President of our new nation it is my duty to maintain national integrity with all possible dignity, especially with those English bast—neighbours watching gleefully to see if we will make a mess of things. So I will not stoop so low as answer in kind McPhee's scurrilous slanders on my own reputation, although how an ex-Dundee Corporation binman has the effrontery to call me a greedy Glasgow windbag is beyond understanding. McPhee calls himself a Leninist but his brand of Leninism is more like neo-cadging . . . lend us this and lend us that. Don't worry, McPhee, once the 1st Battalion has rounded up all those pro-Norwegian traitors in the Orkneys you and your gang will quickly be dealt with.

It has also been brought to my notice that certain viciously seditious elements are going round saying that my own nickname of Backhander Bob stems from corrupt practices in relation to the letting of Glasgow corporation houses. This foul calumny only illustrates the poverty of my opponents' political ideology; simply to put the record straight, at one time I was a school janny in Rutherglen, a job which gave me time to study political theory and macro-sociologicalismics; sometimes the wee hooligans would puff their fags behind the big boiler and I would give then a good-natured back-hander across the lugs. Many of these boys are now responsible, married men and often they come up to me in pubs and say, gratitude shining in their eyes, 'Thank you, Leader, for saving me from a wasted life.'

Having started on a contentious note, I must pay tribute to all the achievements of the first twelve months of our new nationhood. In everything I have been guided by an ideal of harmony and that is why I took on my own shoulders the onerous task of writing all the editorials in the official government newspaper, the *Sunday Post*. All fathers have to be strict at times and that is why I may have appeared harsh when showing the people of Aberdeen the error of hostility towards incorporation in the Greater Northern Council on the grounds that Highlanders are a bunch of idle, drunken dreamers. Remember the old saying—We're all Jock Thamson's bairns?

This must be our goal—unity and harmony. That is why certain books expressing negative, sometimes lewdly worded opinions have been removed from public libraries; a lot of the naive socialism appearing in the poems of our beloved Rabbie Burns served only to denigrate Rabbie's memory and the new, approved edition of his works will obviate the risk of filling young minds with unhelpful ideas. Our oil has made us almost as rich as Sweden but your government here in Glasgow has no intention of emulating the Swedish suicide dimension, individual or national.

In this context I would appeal to those misguided friends in such places as Edinburgh, Perth, Inverness and Oban to reconsider their support for the anti-Glasgow campaign being carried on by a few unscrupulous smalltown charlies wanting only to further their own careers. 'Get Glasgow Off Our Backs' is not a particularly edifying slogan to be seeing in car windows and can only do us harm when we meet in the Councils of Europe to present the case for the mutton pie mountain or the fine malt lake. Surely we are all agreed on the democratic approach to Scottish nationhood? It is not the fault of Glasgow and Clydeside that its voting power has produced a Kelvinhall Front Bench comprised mainly of men from the old Glasgow Corporation Labour caucus.

In time it is my hope that we will have a power-sharing system which will give both the Borders and the crofters and the Perthshire estate-owners a voice on such important committees as the Culture Guidance Advisory Panel, the Alexander Brothers Memorial College Foundation and the Francis Gay Society for Promulgation of Scottish Literature.

While I have no wish to concentrate on matters of a disputatious nature I must just deal here with criticism of your government's decision to conclude a Mutual Aid Treaty with Uganda. In an ever-more complex world we of the small, independent nations must create strong bonds against the vast superpowers and while Field-Marshal Amin has not always shown the greatest wisdom in his handling of the gutter press it has to be remembered he was the first world leader to offer practical help during the bleak years when Scottish independence seemed like a forlorn dream. The exchange of students, cultural ties and a healthy flow of trade between our two emergent nations can only be of benefit to Scotland: Foreign Minister Lord Stein and Chancellor of the Exchequer Lord Fraser go to Uganda next week with all our fervent hopes for a productive conference and a safe return.

And so, at the end of our first twelve months as a fully-fledged member of the community of nations, beset by difficulties yet marching forward with undiminished optimism and the courage that has always marked the Scottish people, I leave you with a message of hope and encouragement. Your government has the will and the men. Let us get on with the job, let us see no more squabbling and backbiting and Scotland will prosper. Goodnight to you all, in the far islands and in the glens and the great industrial conurbations. Scotland for ever!

How did it sound, Jimmy? You think my bald patch looked shiny under these lights? Come on away to the VIP lounge, my face will fall off if I don't get a big dram intae it.

"Don't worry about me, I always get like this
when I hear the pipes."

Scenes from the Scottish Republic

Everyday life in post-independence Scotland, as depicted by official artist KEN TAYLOR

"Typically sneaky of the Scots . . . disband their armed forces . . . make the place a tax-haven and leave us to defend their border for them . . ."

". . . of course we'd be delighted to accept your deposit of £500,000 in English money . . . we want to encourage the small saver . . ."

". . . That? That's Aberdeen
Mean Time . . ."

120

"May it Please Your Scots Lordship . . ."

FENTON BRESLER looks at Scottish Law

I AM all for being proud of your country and proud of your calling, but Scottish lawyers really do carry it to excess. According to Regius Professor David M. Walker of Glasgow University, the Scottish legal system is "largely indigenous nor yet narrowly parochial nor yet insular." Another Scots law professor, T. B. Smith, QC, has told an overwhelmingly English lecture audience. "I shall not conceal from you my conviction that an impartial arbiter would prefer solutions of Scottish law to those of English law."

And a distinguished Scottish judge, Lord Cooper, has confidently written, "The Scottish legal tradition is a thing to be prized both in Scotland and beyond its borders."

The galling thing is that they are 100% correct. Scots law—based on a somewhat odd amalgam of ancient Roman Law and sturdy Northern common sense—is frequently more enlightened, simple and straightforward than what we have to put up with south of the Border. Whenever there is a significant "reform" in English law, you'll often find that we are only starting to do what the Scots have been doing for centuries. "Are we for ever to be behind Scotland?" Lord Denning, Master of the Rolls and senior English Appeal Court judge, has asked.

Look at this list:

● In England, we are terribly proud of the fact that in 1949 the two major political parties for once got together and passed the Legal Aid and Advice Act, introducing State legal aid. "The little man's charter to the courts of England," Sir Hartley Shawcross hailed it. But a system of free legal aid for the poor has existed in Scotland since 1424. And in 1587 it was enacted that all those accused of crime should be legally represented: a state of affairs they only got around to in the United States of America a few years ago in the hotly-criticised U.S. Supreme Court decision in *Gideon v. Wainwright,* which almost got Chief Justice Earl Warren impeached.

● In 1926, England at last passed an Act allowing for "legitimation by subsequent marriage." If unmarried parents subsequently marry, their child becomes legitimate. A great breakthrough in post-World War One England. That has been the law in Scotland—stemming directly from a Roman Law principle—since time immemorial.

● In 1937, England—relentlessly prodded by A. P. (Sir Alan) Herbert—daringly introduced desertion as a ground for divorce. You have been able to get a divorce for desertion in Scotland since 1573.

● In 1938, England passed an Act preventing a man cutting his wife or family out of his will. Nowadays, William Shakespeare could not leave Anne Hathaway his second-best bed. He would have to make "reasonable provision" for her. In Scotland—through another ancient Roman principle—a man's family is entitled, as of right, to a fixed proportion of part of his assets.

And so on. And so on. You name a recent legal reform—majority verdicts for juries, non-publicity for magistrates' court hearings in major crimes, no more last-minute "alibi" defences, "diminished responsibility" as a partial defence in murder cases—and the Scots got there first. We have merely been copying them.

In fact, the Scots are pretty angry at what they say *we* are doing to *their* law. A predominantly English Parliament in London makes new laws governing everyday life in Scotland—although sometimes the English legislators are surprisingly understanding of Northern vagaries. The "Wolfenden" legislation legalising consenting male adults in private has tactfully not been extended to Scotland.

And in all civil cases—though not in criminal cases—the highest court of appeal is the House of Lords, where Scottish law lords are in a permanent minority.

"Thanks to a predominantly English legislature and a mainly English court of last resort, the integrity of the Law of Scotland is often seriously strained," complains Professor Andrew Gibb, QC, in his "Preface to Scots Law."

The trouble is—so runs the theory—that the English law lords just do not understand what makes Scots law, or the Scots people, tick. "Mandarins from south of the Border," they have been described as.

Some years ago, a Scots woman tried to divorce her husband for cruelty. He had often been rude to her, threatened her in front of their children, humiliated her, threatened to throw her down the stairs of their house and generally brought her to such a low ebb that she had tried to kill herself. The Scots courts refused her a decree. Said the Lord President of the Court of Session, the highest Scottish judge: "Whether it be that the Scottish character is of tougher fibre or of blunter susceptibilities, or that the Calvinist tradition still finds expression in a deeper sanctity of the marriage tie and its obligations, the fact remains that more than one decree on the ground of cruelty has recently been pronounced in England, which would not have been granted in Scotland."

The woman appealed to the House of Lords—and the Lord President's ruling was reversed. "I can find no difference between the law of Scotland and England in this respect," said Lord Tucker, of solidly English legal experience. Concurring with his three fellow law lords two of whom were Scotsmen!

Chauvinism can sometimes go to surprising lengths. In an English murder trial in the early nineteen-sixties an American serviceman was acquitted after explaining that he had strangled the dead girl while asleep—and woke up to find his hands round her throat. Two days later, he disposed of the body in a ditch. Mr. Justice Glyn Jones asked if there was any record of such a defence, and was apparently told there was none. Professor T. B. Smith, QC, proudly claims in his lectures on "British Justice: The Scottish Contributions": "There had been in Scotland."

In 1878—again, the Scots beat us by nearly a century—a man named Fraser, while asleep, believed himself to be attacked by a wild animal—and woke up to find he had killed his eighteen-month-old child. His penalty: he was discharged on undertaking to sleep alone in future. Comments Professor Smith: "This precedent might have been useful to Mr. Justice Glyn Jones. It may be regretted that the American serviceman's discharge was not, as in Fraser's case, conditional on his undertaking to sleep alone." A somewhat unworldly suggestion for an American serviceman on leave in this country, some may think.

Yet all is not sunshine and light and staunch Scots pride. The famous—or notorious—Scots jury verdict of "Not proven" has been described to me by a cynical Scots lawyer as meaning: "We think you did it. But it's not proved. So get the hell out of here!"

And very recently, Scottish lawyers, angered at the meanness of their senior judges when awarding damages in serious personal injury cases, called for changes in Scots law to—of all things!—bring awards into line with those in England. In a recent Scots case, for instance, a 46-year-old married woman paralysed in a road accident had first a £23,000 and then a £22,000 damages award quashed by the Scottish appeal court as being "excessive." Eventually, she settled for £10,000. In England, those same injuries would have been worth £15,000 to £20,000. In a strongly worded memorandum to the Scottish Law Commission, the Council of the Law Society of Scotland said they viewed this situation with "grave disquiet."

You can hardly blame English lawyers for smirking quietly to themselves. Few would ever be so outspoken—or so inaccurate—as to refer, in English Lord Chancellor Lord Maugham's, words to "those interesting relics of barbarism, tempered by a few importations from Rome, known to the world as Scots Law." But it is pleasant sometimes to get your own back. It makes a welcome change from continually being looked down upon—with whatever justification.

LIFE IN SCOTLAND

The five-foot-tall Pakistani whose middle-man role in a £3,000m international financial deal has brought the Australian government to the brink of collapse is known as "Wee Peter" to his neighbours in a Paisley cul-de-sac. *(Glasgow Herald)*

IV

MACBETH
How now, you (background
   interference) hags,
What is't you do?
3rd WITCH
Scale of dragon, tooth of wolf,
(Unintelligible) gulf,
(Technical disturbance) hence,
(Harmless ethnic inference).
Purposes so far from laudable,
Something (expletive) (inaudible).
MACBETH
Then live, Macduff. What need I fear
   of thee?
But yet I'll (unintelligible) be.

Who broke into Duncan's room? Who covered up the Banquo caper?
Is Macduff telling the truth? Where was Malcolm? Is the King of
Scotland a crook? Here at last are

THE MACBETH TAPES

prepared and edited by HANDELSMAN

I

MACBETH
Is this (inaudible) I see before me,
The handle toward my hand? Come, let
   me clutch thee!
I have thee not, and yet (inaudible).
I go, and it is (unintelligible).
Hear it not, Duncan, for it is
   (inaudible).
That summons thee to heaven, or to
   (expletive).

III

MACBETH
Which of you have done this?
LORDS   What, my good lord?
MACBETH
Thou canst not say I did it. Never shake
Thy (characterization omitted) locks
   at me.
ROSS   Gentlemen, rise.
His Highness is (inaudible).
LADY MACBETH
   Sit, worthy friends.
My lord is often (unintelligible).

V

LADY MACBETH
Out, (characterization omitted) spot!
Out, I say! Who would have thought
the old man to have had so much
(unintelligible) in him? What, will
these hands ne'er be (inaudible)?

VI

MACBETH   I will not yield,
To kiss the (unintelligible) feet,
Though Birnam Wood be come to
   Dunsinane,
And thou opposed, being of no
   (inaudible),
Yet I will (18 minute hum). Macduff,
And (tape ran out) that first cries
   "Hold, enough!"

VII

MACDUFF   Hail, (gap)! Behold
where stands
Th' (inaudible)'s (characterization
   omitted) head.
MACBETH
This newest crisis hath me near
   defeated!
I'll tough it out, and (expletive deleted).

II

MACBETH
Was it not yesterday we spoke
   together?
(CHARACTERIZATIONS OMITTED)
It was, so please your Highness.
MACBETH   Well then, now
(Inaudible) predominant in your nature
That (unintelligible) common eye
For sundry weighty reasons.
2nd (CHARACTERIZATION OMITTED)
   We shall, my lord,
Perform what you command us.
MACBETH
Your spirits (unintelligible) flight,
If it find heaven, must (inaudible)
   tonight.

The New
Scottish Parliament

Extracts from the first session

The Hoose o' Parliament sat at 2.30 p.m. The Hame Secretary, the Rt. Hon. Murdoch Lothian, rose to move the Scottish Postage Stamp Enabling Bill.

MR. LOTHIAN (Stirling, Nationalist Tory)—As you know . . . (Various cries of "Wheest!", "Losh, man!" and "Whaur's your Scots the noo?") . . . As ye ken fine, our Parliament has full and independent powers except in such cases as it conflicts with that at Westminster. In practice, this limits us to a small range of activities. We could not, even if we wished, declare war on Russia, or even Iceland, by ourselves. (Cry of "Could we invade England?") Nor do we have the power to construct a rival to Concorde or resite the Chunnel under the Firth of Forth, for which I think we are all grateful. What we *do* have the power to do is take advantage of those money-raising projects which until now have been open to the English government alone.

MR. WENTWORTH (Morningside, English Nationalist)—Point of order. It is the British government.

MR. LOTHIAN—I bow to the superior knowledge of our honourable member of the English Nationalist party, and congratulate him on the speed with which he is mastering our outlandish accent. (Laughter.) For many years the Post Office in London has made considerable profits from printing pictorial stamps commemorating such vital events as the Battle of Hastings and the foundation of the Salvation Army. Personally, I welcomed the Battle of Hastings stamps, celebrating as they did a great victory for our Norman allies, but the time has now come for us to print Scottish commemorative postage stamps which will not only commemorate great Scottish landmarks but also bring in the loot. This bill which is before you enables us to do precisely that.

MR. HAMISH McLEOD (Outer Isles, Hebridean Home Rule Party) said, in Gaelic, that he hoped there would be a pictorial series glorifying the wool industry of the Isles and that he personally knew a little man in Skye who would produce it in glowing colours at a fraction of the cost of the profiteers in Glasgow.

MR. LOTHIAN—While awaiting a translation of that contribution, I would like to announce that the first series of Scottish stamps would commemorate the most outstanding victories of past years over England. We envisage a 1p

Bannockburn, a 2p Stirling Bridge, 3p Prestonpans, and a $3\frac{1}{2}$p stamp showing Charles Edward in Derby.

MR. ALASTAIR GRIEVE (St. Andrews, Scottish Academic Party) wanted to know whit aboot the 9p stamp.

MR. LOTHIAN—I was coming to that. It will show the victorious Scottish football team which won our place in Munich. (Cheers, singing and a bottle from the backbenches.) I have now been handed a translation from the honourable member from the Outer Isles. Does he mean to say that the stamp itself should be made of wool?

MR. McLEOD said in Gaelic that he would await a translation of the question into the native Scottish language before answering it.

MR. LOTHIAN said he was not sure from the honourable member's expression what his reaction was but that he would look forward to a translation.

MR. McLEOD said in Gaelic that was all right by him.

MR. LOTHIAN—Whatever that means.

MR. IAIN FARQUHAR (Inverness West, Highland Home Industries Export Campaign Party)—It seems a damned shame that we should be following the English example so closely. Should we not launch forth bravely into the first tartan stamps on the market? Was there not a case for advertising on the stamps, if they were big enough? In my constituency alone I can think of a dozen craftsmen who could turn out large postage stamps saying "Come to Sunny Nairn, Jewel of the Moray Firth 3p", with a list of recommended hotels.

MR. TOM LOWRIE (Kelso, Lowlands-For-The-Lowlanders Movement) asked what was so damned good about a holiday in the Highlands, where people were notoriously arrogant and almost equally lazy, when visitors could have the time of their life in the only civilised part of Scotland, which he did not think he needed to point out was the area south of a line drawn between Glasgow and Edinburgh.

MR. J. O'BRIEN (Mount Vernon, Glasgow, Presbyterian) said he thought that it was an admirable suggestion to draw a line between Glasgow and Edinburgh, and the sooner they were isolated from the effete snobs in Edinburgh the better.

MR. DUNCAN CAMPBELL (Edinburgh, North-West, Scottish Culture Party) said how pleased he was personally to hear someone from Glasgow using such sophisticated, long words as "isolated" and "the", and that if Glaswegians matured at this rate they might even have a decent building in their town before the century was out.

MR. McPHERSON said that he would not take that kind of talk from anyone and that it was about time Mr. Campbell got a good hiding.

SPEAKER—Please refer to him correctly.

MR. McPHERSON apologised and said that it was about time the honourable member got a good hiding.

MR. CAMPBELL—That'll be the day. You're all puff and wind.

MR. McPHERSON said he would show him about that.

MR. CAMPBELL asked the honourable member from Paisley to leave go, as he was breaking his arm (Cries of "Shame!" and "Put the boot in".)

126

MR. LOTHIAN restored order and asked for any other questions.

THE LAIRD OF AUCHTERFEWIE (Highlands Central, Stuart Restoration Party) asked if there were any plans to delete the head of the Hanoverian Queen of England's head from the stamps and insert the rightful head of Charles III, sometimes erroneously known as Bonnie Prince Charlie.

MR. FERGUS FITZPAYNE (Glasgow Central, Sauchiehall Street Movement) said there had been no mention so far of the great Scottish industrialists—Dunlop, Macadam, Macintosh. (Cry of "What about Macchiavelli, then?")

MR. LAURENCE BLAIR-OLIPHANT (Blairgowrie, Come-To-Perthshire-For-Your-Holidays Movement) said that he didn't know much about postage stamps but that he remembered from his childhood preferring stamps with funny shapes and would it not be possible to produce a series making use of the outlines of Scottish counties or would this make it difficult to perforate them, also the Orkneys might be tricky.

MR. SANDY BUCHANAN (Ayr, Cleaner Golf Party) said he had a good idea which he had now forgotten.

MR. ALEX HAMILTON (Gretna Green, Improve-The-Image-Of-Gretna-Green Party) wondered if anyone had heard the story about the Japanese tourist and the kilt.

MR. ROSS THOMSON (Upper Tay, Highland Fishing) said he hadn't, but he knew a damned good song about a poacher and his wife.

MR. LOTHIAN said that if nobody had any further questions about the Scottish Postage Stamp Enabling Bill, he would move for a division. The Bill was passed by 245 to 3, 1 abstaining (Mr. Muir, Temperance Party). The House then proceeded to a debate on the Repatriation of Immigrants (London Scottish) Bill.

LIFE IN SCOTLAND

An invoice for £11·83 issued by North East Fife District Council to an Anstruther woman for the hire of Cellardyke Town Hall, for a going-away party, has been written off. All reminders have been returned marked "gone away". *(Fife Herald News)*

A man broke into a Kirkcaldy warehouse four times in a matter of days. He told the police when he was caught—"I came down from Mars right through the roof for a can of McEwans." *(Dundee Evening Telegraph)*

To get an indication of the weather conditions, a coastguard on the spot was asked to estimate the wind speed. He was sorry, he replied, but he didn't have a gauge. However, if it was any help, the wind had just blown his Land-Rover over a cliff. *(Aberdeen Evening Express)*

TARTAN TAKE OVER:
The Biggest Oil Threat Yet!

If Scots Nationalists seize the North Sea oil profits, estimated at £4,000 million a year by 1980, what will happen to England? And to Scotland? These extracts from the newspaper files of three years hence are far from reassuring.

From the Daily Express

THE WORST CITY IN THE WORLD

(By Clapham Bowser)

Today I hopped on my left foot into the Wicked City of Wick, the fabled Gomorrah of the North, the blackest sink of infamy since Port Royal, Jamaica was engulfed in an earthquake.

My right foot had been cut off by drunken Excisemen at the Border.

Here in Wick debauched tinkers richer than Croesus boast of breaking all Ten Commandments before breakfast. The old law which forbids the giving away of women as Bingo prizes is openly defied.

Outside the harbour the luxury yachts of drillers from Cromarty lie at anchor. They cannot enter because the port is choked with Cadillacs, many of them with their drowned drivers still at the wheel, the victims of murderous sprees.

Scenes like these are the price Scotland pays for her new-found wealth in the North Sea—wealth she refuses to share with her ancient enemy, England.

I was told that in Wick surgeons can no longer perform operations, even when they are sober, because revellers have stolen the last reserves of blood at unholy altars.

"It is the greatest hangover in our unhappy history, but at last we have found ourselves as a nation." The speaker, who described himself as the Moderator of the Free Church of Scotland, applied a match to the potion in the skull he was holding and drank the contents flaming.

"D'ye recognise the skull?" he asked me, as he extinguished his beard. "Aye, it's Harold Wilson's. He tried to nationalise oor oil, ye ken."

Outside rose hellish cackles as bands of ruffians and their drabs hanged each other on the lampposts.

"If he thinks this is bad," said the self-styled Moderator, "ye should hiv bin here at Hogmanay. Here, laddie, drink this. Let me light it for you."

I made an excuse and left.

Free-spending oil workers relax with their tiara-topped women at "The Jolly Calvin," the vast recreational complex covering one hundred acres at John o' Groats, "Las Vegas of the North."

From The Daily Telegraph

OIL TYCOONS ORDER CLEARANCES

THE Scots have long memories *(writes our Property and Estates Correspondent)*. All over England the new oil tycoons from the North are buying up big estates and driving out the impoverished inhabitants to make room for sheep. This is their belated revenge for the Highland "clearances" of last century.

"The real difficulty is to distinguish Englishmen from sheep," joked Jock McCarfare, president of the mammoth Tartan Oils. He has just acquired Chatsworth, ancestral home of the Dukes of Devonshire. "Some of the estate workers were slow to move," he said, "but they soon shifted after my agents put a torch to their roof timbers."

Mr McCarfare is having a giant granite statue of himself built on the highest peak in Derbyshire, rivalling the one erected at Golspie to the Duke of Sutherland who emptied the Scottish glens.

Mr Mick McGarble, who heads the £2,000 million Caithness Oil Consortium, told me: "I have just been looking over Lancashire, which seems to me a county suited neither to sheep nor men, so I propose to turn it into a deer forest. There will be a number of well-paid jobs for ghillies, if they keep their noses clean."

Asked what he proposed to do about Liverpool, he said: "There is no room for sentiment in these matters. It will have to go."

From The Guardian

ENGLAND ON HER KNEES

The days when England will be no more than a despised puppet of Scotland are rapidly nearing (*writes our Political Correspondent*). It is not inconceivable that the affairs of "South Britain" will be settled in a couple of afternoons every year by the Edinburgh Parliament, thus reversing completely the system which has hitherto existed.

It is even possible that the other nations of the European Economic Community will be taking their orders from Scotland, once the difficult problems of communicating with the "Arabs in Kilts" have been overcome.

With her stranglehold on the two most precious liquids known to man—oil and whisky—Scotland is now the most powerful nation in the West.

Under the newly-concluded Gleneagles Treaties, oil from the North Sea piped to Scotland is supplied only to those nations willing to concede moral, intellectual and spiritual superiority to the Scots. This poses a cruel challenge to the conscience of civilised man, but the choice is inescapable. The more oil a nation needs, the more Burns Nights it will have to hold.

Unofficially the Westminster Parliament has let it be known that it is willing to truckle and cringe without reserve. If the Scots demand a restoration of the Stuart dynasty, or the universal adoption of the glottal stop, it is unlikely that any serious obstacles will be put in their way.

NEWS IN BRIEF

Among would-be tourists turned away by the Scottish immigration authorities at Gretna yesterday was Mr Paul Getty, at one time the richest oil man in the world. Officials were not satisfied that he had sufficient funds to maintain himself.

• •

On the field of Bannockburn the former memorial commemorating the Scots victory over the English has been replaced by a 100-ft gold obelisk, from the top of which leaps an Eternal Flame, fuelled by North Sea oil.

• •

No further bulletins are being issued about the Loch Ness Monster, which has recovered from oil poisoning contracted after its recent escape into the North Sea.

• •

Mr Hughie McTooth, the well-known public house drag artiste and street busker, has been appointed the first Lord Rector of Oxford University.

Believing that the dying city of London is sitting on limitless reserves of oil, Scots prospectors—not content with their North Sea bonanza—have erected this giant rig in Piccadilly Circus (note Eros statue). Hardly a word of protest has been voiced by apathetic Londoners.

From The Daily Mirror

FAN'S TRAIL OF HAVOC

THOUSANDS of fabulously rich Scots football fans roared into Heathrow yesterday in their executive jets. At one time the aircraft were so thick that they darkened the sun.

The chaos was such that all international flights were grounded for twelve hours.

At the airport the tam-o'-shantered fans were mobbed by well-dressed Englishmen begging alms.

"Ye didna want to know us when we came by coach and were sick all over the Underground," said a fan from Aberdeen, tossing a bundle of fivers contemptuously into the crowd.

The Scots piled into taxis for Wembley, but most cabs ran out of petrol before they were half way there and their occupants missed the Cup Final.

"It's a reet poverty-stricken country," said Rob McKeeler, a pipe-layer from "Millionaires' Row," Peterhead. "Why can ye no' find oil fur yersels?"

On their return flight to the North the fans buzzed every town and village in their path, stampeded herds of cattle and tried to set fire to forests with home-made incendiary bombs. "It was like a thousand-bomber raid gone berserk," said a police official.

"Even Everton fans were never like this," remarked a Football Association spokesman. "But if we want our trickle of oil from the North, we must learn to live with it."

Former Clydeside Red rebel and television philosopher, Jimmy ("The Sheikh") Reid, Scotland's £250,000-a-year overlord, has a spending problem. "We've built houses, schools, hospitals, nurseries, gaols, universities, motorways, recreation centres and marinas," he says, "and now it looks as though we'll have to start putting up office blocks for the bosses." No wonder Jim looks grim.

The Oil Rush

ALAN COREN and HEWISON,
back from the Scottish Klondike, report

THE VISION

IT was, as I remember, a drear drizzling Tuesday in early February when the hitherto unspoken Dream was first articulated.

I had been pacing the unlovely corridors of the Tudor Street offices, staring at the forefingers from which long years of comic typing had erased the whorls, when I bumped against the gaunt frame of William Hewison who was similarly engaged. His eyes were what Barbara Cartland would call hollow, and his thin hands were ingrained with the giveaway stigmata of Indian ink which set the cartoonist apart from ordinary men.

We looked at one another for some time.

"We have been out here too long," I said. "All this humorous rubbish, all this joke-writing and pencilling of funny faces, what is it all for? Is it, I put it to you, man's work? We grow flabby in mind and body, lad! There are frontiers still to be crossed, and wastes to be charted, and fortunes to be made by guts and sweat, and big women to be waylaid!"

He thought for a while, his fine face creased with the effort to grasp it all.

"How big?" he said, at last.

"I am talking," I said, "about oil! Less than a thousand miles due north of here, Hewison, there is a new Yukon. Strong men with tattooed forearms stand poised to suck millions in black gold from the earth's crust. It is like California in 1849, Hewison, like Alaska in 1890, all is boom and rush and ruthlessness and money, and men prepared to seize the day will be carrying the stuff home in lorries! Let us grab a couple of shovels, and trek north!"

"You have to be a company," said Hewison. "I read it somewhere. You can't just row out into the North Sea and start digging."

"You miss the point," I replied. "Or, rather, points. First, if there is oil under the sea, there is no reason why there should not also be oil under the land, nor any why we should not therefore look for it. Second, even if it is not there, think of the ancillary delights of the region! Why, I have heard of mushrooming casinos, of truckloads of lithe women disembarking every hour on the hour for the accommodation of the big spenders currently flocking to Nigg Bay to work upon the rigs, of wild nights of music, love and single malts! And third, what

Dr. WILLIAM C. HEWISON
D.Sc., F.G.S., Mem. OAC(Kuwait)

Research Division,
Anglo-Bahraini Oil Co.,
Bahrain, P.G.

Telex BAH 265863 (Aboil)
Tel: 78199

Dr. ALAN COREN
D.Sc., F.Inst.Geol., Dip. de Petro-Chimie

Research Division,
Anglo-Bahraini Oil Co.,
Bahrain, P.G.

Telex BAH 265863 (Aboil)
Tel: 78199

might we not learn, Hewison, of human greed and human lust and even human worth, out there on the last frontier?"

"We may write a new *Eskimo Nell!*" he cried, suddenly. "With erotic illustrations! They never," he muttered, "let me draw smut here. A million copies in paperback, American rights, a film, a television series, a . . ."

I looked away, as he rambled. Already, I reflected, the terrible magic of black gold was manifesting its weird power to twist men's minds.

WE PREPARE FOR OUR JOURNEY

At the top of the page, you will see the cards we had printed as evidence of our bona (mala?) fides. They were to gain us entrée to the privy cabals of the oil trade. Further to these, we obtained Wellington boots, thick gloves, and parkas with myriad zips; and our Equipment.

Now, one cannot look for oil as one looks for gold, i.e. by walking to where it might be, taking a baking dish off your donkey, and dipping it in the nearest rill. Along the Moray Firth, Walter Brennan would call up derision of a hysterical

131

order. However, what you do need costs around eight million pounds, and this kind of loot not being readily to hand in the humour business, we chose instead to weld a poker to a trickle-charger, solder a pair of earphones to its other end, and borrow a mine-detector, the modus operandi being to wander about with the mine-detector, hammer the poker in with sudden decision, don the earphones, and watch the dial of the trickle-charger for some exhilarating response.

That none ever comes will be scant surprise to the senior geologists among you. However, as 99·99% of the Scottish population knows nothing of how preliminary explorations for oil are made, our kit and technique were rather impressive; and had the other ·01% strolled up to enquire as to our activities, we should merely have withdrawn our poker and wellied away at high speed.

We also had some mind-boggling charts, forged by Hewison's expert nib, showing Ross & Cromarty in meticulous bogus detail, right down to the latest onshore evidence of rich oil deposits, as carried out by earlier fake surveys from Anglo-Bahreini. I, for my literary part, had invented an impenetrable Joycean technological jargon with which to numb the minds of the curious.

The function of this agglomerated junk was multifold: if there was indeed oil about, our suspicious activities might winkle out the information from those who genuinely knew, thus making it the cheapest method of prospecting; if there was none, then our quest to examine human motives under field conditions might be richly rewarded anyhow, as men strove to get in on our act; and whether there was any or not, it would be quite clear that we were oil men, and therefore in the market for big women.

THE QUEST BEGINS

The Euston sleeper deposited us in Inverness on a slatey dawn, out of which we drove due north in a hired Land Rover. Not that we had any intention of driving

DAY 2 – NIGG. Afternoon.
We consult an Oil-Man.

"Me—I'm a Greek. Catering staff. I tell you—the boys all love my little bouzouki."

132

anywhere that could not be reached by more urbane transport; but in the prospecting business, nothing matches the Land Rover for rugged probity.

We put ourselves to our first test at Invergordon, a town which sounds as though it ought to contain more than 2,108 souls, especially as most of these, from a cursory glance along its one main street, are solicitors. It was to the most imposing of these premises that we presented ourselves, having first ascertained from the local bank that there were no estate agents in the region, and that anyone interested in the acquisition of land would have to make his enquiries through a solicitor, via whom the purchase of same would have to pass.

There were, amazingly, six citizens in the waiting-room, a traffic unprecedented in my own long experience of the law, and given the number of law offices we had already passed, one might be forgiven for thinking that the major industry and pastime of the town was litigation. I approached the chill receptionist.

"I wonder if I might see . . ."

"There's a queue," she said, nodding curtly to the assemblage of divorcees, slanderers, axe-murderers, or whatever.

I slid my card across.

It is usually only in the cheaper novelettes that changes come over people.

"Och, ye're wi' Anglo-Bahreini!" she simpered, while I reflected upon the speed with which our great company's reputation had travelled in the four days since I had invented it. She pressed her intercom button.

"Sorry tae interrupt ye when ye're wi' a client," she cooed, "but I have Dr. Coren of Anglo-Bahreini Oil here, and . . ."

The intercom squawked, and a far door banged, and the image of Willie Whitelaw appeared before us, beckoning us humbly to an ante-room. I explained briefly that we wanted to know of any available land in the area, and he wanted to know if it was for industrial or residential development, and I said no; we couldn't commit ourselves, of course, but we had done some preliminary hot-shaft sub-igneous spot probings, and there seemed a strong possibility that . . . and here Hewison unrolled his tantalising chart, with its arrowed myths of subterranean goodies, and rolled it up again, quickly.

Into the lawyer's eyes there came a light which left Wolf Rock at the post.

"I've all these people tae see, ye ken," he murmured apologetically. "May I suggest ye come out to my hoose and have dinner wi' me tonight? I always find an informal atmosphere so much more conducive tae business, d'ye no find that yourself, ha-ha-ha?"

We assured him we would ring to confirm after we had seen one or two of his colleagues (which dented his smile somewhat), and left.

The receptionist leapt to open the door for us. The six clients stared bitterly.

DOWN BELOW

North along the Cromarty Firth we travelled, and as we travelled we stopped, here and there, and sprang with businesslike and extravagant urgency from the Land Rover, and unloaded our gear and strapped on our electro-geoseismic rubbish and our headphones and hammered in Mrs. Hewison's poker and shouted our readings to one another and noted them on our clipboards and took bearings of our position and checked them against our charts; and everywhere small knots of people gathered, fighting their curiosity, the pluckier finally asking us whether we were from the council/the Government/the Rates Office, and was it about the new road, or foot-and-mouth, or this or that; and when we demurred, and got ourselves deliberately trapped, and finally, shamefacedly, admitted that we were looking for oil, the mystic word rippled from lip to lip, and everyone told everyone else that they had told them so for years, that it stood tae reason.

And when we asked them, yes, more than one of them had heard rumblings underground, yes, they had smelt the smell we described in the air on warm wet mornings, yes, there had been other groups of mysterious men through during the past year, and yes, they *had* heard strange bangs in the middle of the night and yes, they *were* like two rifle shots fired in quick succession.

And I would nod at Hewison, and he would nod at me, and one or other of us would say:

"Deep pluvio-stratal echo-implosion soundings, I thought as much, that confirms it!"

And always in the rear-view mirror as we drove away, the groups would watch us out of sight.

With never a soul, not one, to raise the point of the possible despoliation of this lovely land, the disruption of its society an onshore oil-boom would bring, the radical changes in its way of life.

A lot of them wanted to look at our charts, though, to try to discover what their house might be sitting on.

THE BIG WOMEN (PART ONE)
We stopped that night at the Royal Hotel in Tain, on the south shore of the Dornoch Firth and a dozen miles north of Nigg itself. There was no-one to carry our bags up.

"Aye, the staff is all awa' tae Nigg!" cried the manageress bitterly. "I lost three chambermaids last week alone!"

"You see!" I exclaimed to the dispirited Hewison (we had seen almost nothing but men the entire day) at dinner, "All the women are at Nigg as I foretold! Believe me, Hewison, I am no stranger to the silver screen, I know what it will be like, they will be clad in fishnet and scarlet taffeta, with black velvet bands around their lovely throats to set off their embonpoint, their golden hair will be piled high upon their heads and fixed with rhinestone-studded combs, they will reek of irresistible cheap perfume and wish to know what the boys in the backroom will have, they will dance on the tables, flashing their garters, and when they hear that the twin-spearhead of the famed Anglo-Bahreini Oil Company is in town they will enmesh their slim fingers in our hair and lead us to rooms with mirrors in the ceilings!"

"Oh good," said Hewison.

DAY 3 — GOLSPIE. Afternoon.
We probe the links.

I splashed on a lot of Monsieur Rochas after dinner, and gargled as much Listerine, and buffed my gold cuff-links to painful iridescence, and went to get Hewison.

But it had been a long day, and much as I hammered on his door, he would not wake up.

THE BIG WOMEN (PART TWO)

So we drove to Nigg the next morning. In the icy mist of the flat foreshore, giant cranes were building one another. A half-erected oil-rig lay on its side, twinkling at strategic points as welders cleaved to their bright task. All this went on behind high wire fences, whose rare gates were manned by security guards; occasionally these moaned open to let in or out charabancs filled with men in yellow helmets.

We decided to follow one of these to the town of Nigg.

It is a long, low building in dirty white stucco, with weeds round it. Beside it lies moored a grey boat the size of a Channel ferry, called the *Highland Queen*.

The town itself was closed, although we rang twice, and from the boat issued a line of the yellow-helmeted men who formed a permanent shuffling queue for the continually departing charas.

We approached an inhabitant who was sitting beside his 1100 in the fog, listening to bouzouki music on his in-car stereo. He had that fearful pallor which is left when alien cold drains the face of its natural swarthiness. He nodded when we asked him if this was all there was of booming Nigg.

"De mens live on de boat," he said. "I yam cook."

"Are there, er, women?" I enquired.

"No wimmins," he said.

"What does everyone do, then?"

"De mens weld," said the Greek cook, "and in de nights she is open de house," he nodded towards the building, "and de mens get drunk."

"Scarlet taffeta," muttered Hewison, "garters. Mirrors in the ceiling."

"Wotty say?" asked the cook.

"It doesn't matter," I said.

EPILOGUE

In the days that followed before we turned south once more for home, these examples were frequently replicated. The dreaded cashflow grippe had struck down many a brave developer, and much of the land snapped up at the beginning of the boom three years ago was back on the market; we were offered everything from solitary crofts to a six-hundred acre parcel with a castle on it that had been converted into executive offices at enormous expense, for executives that had never showed. And everywhere we were assured that whatever ravages we wished to wreak could be wrought unimpeded.

We learned some interesting things: for example, there may very well be onshore oil in just those places where we flew our preposterous kites (this from a professor of geology), that we could buy the land under which it might be, and that there was every likelihood (this from a county planning officer in Dingwall) that we would get permission to extract it. So that there is no reason why Texaco and BP and Conoco and all the rest should enjoy a monopoly: the old Texan dream of a gusher in the backyard may be dreamt here, with a solid chance of realisation.

I prefer, however, to address myself to the resident professional at Dornoch Golf Club. He is the only man we met to whom we wish to apologise. Having allowed us to explore his lovely links, he came out to stop us as we packed to drive away.

"I hope to God you found nothing," he said. "They've played golf here for, oh, two hundred years. Would you dig all this up for a few barrels of oil?"

Not us, lad. But we can only speak for Anglo-Bahreini.

"They might fool the Procurator Fiscal at Dornock but they certainly don't fool me."

Chapter Eight

Home and away: the Scots in exile, and out of it

The great westward movement of tribes across Europe over the years resulted in the Scots finding themselves trapped in a wet, misty cul-de-sac in the northern half of Britain with nowhere left to go except the Orkneys and Shetlands. As this seemed a poor solution, most of them have taken a deep breath and gone on to Canada, New Zealand, Australia, Samoa, the Far East and even, in desperate cases, London, where they have formed Caledonian societies and become even more fiercely Scottish than before. They turn out en masse twice a year, once for Burns Night and once for Billy Connolly's world tour.

This final section contains some home thoughts from abroad, some glimpses of what they might be missing at home and a tribute or two to the culture the Scots have taken with them. For further details on that other great group of Scottish exiles, Celtic and Rangers fans stranded abroad, see the chapter on Sport.

Scotland for the Scots

is all very well; but when they get Home Rule and the return of millions of anglicized Scotsmen, how will they cope?

"Bloody nouveau scotch!"

"Poor Fiona, having to go out to work—she's got five engineers and three doctors to support now!"

*"Bluidy typical, they gie the job to the fella
wearing the Old Etonian tartan tie!"*

"It's no use, Jock, we can't compete against London know-how."

Maintainin' Oor Prestige

R. S. McLELLAN

"AH wis readin' a bit in the papers whaur it says the country owes a lot tae the Merchant Service."

"Jist that," remarked Peter.

"It said that if it wasnae for the grub oor ships bring in we'd a' be starvin' in a matter o' weeks."

"Nae doot, McNidder; but tak' it frae me that's no a' the country owes tae the Merchant Service. Ah've naething tae say against Naval officers, an' Ah saw a guid lot o' them a while back, but they're no' in it wi' oor ain officers when it comes tae keepin' up the prestige o' the auld country.

"There's nae braggin' or boastin', mind ye; jist a natural demonstration o' the stamina an' endurance o' oor prood island race. Nae effort aboot it; it's a' part o' the day's work wi' them. Ah mind a case in point.

"It happened a wheen o' years back, when Ah wis bosun o' a fower-masted barque. We were lyin' in a Dago port, an' wan nicht the second mate, the third mate an' masel' were up toon in yin o' thae cafés. In a wind-ship, Ah micht tell ye, it's nae disgrace for the mates tae hae a drink wi' the bosun, provided he's a sailor an' no' a puddin'.

"We'd had no' a bad evenin', wan way an' anither, and it wis gettin' latish when in cam' three Dago officers—sojers, no' sailors. They'd nae English an' we didna savvy their lingo, but onybody kens the signs for a drink. In a wee while we were a' like brithers.

"By-and-by yin o' the Dagoes got up an' gied us a song. When he'd feenished we could see frae the looks o' them that it wis up tae us, so the third mate, a wee Cockney like a bit o' steel wire, got up an' sang 'The Lights o' the 'arbour.' Everybody wis satisfied, so we had anither drink. That's whit ye ca' the *entente cordiale*.

"Dagoes aye seem to get mair an' mair patriotic as the nicht goes on, an' it wisnae lang afore the three o' them jumped up an' sang their National Anthem wi' due solemnity. That kind o' disconcertit us, for Britishers, ye'll mind, hate tae be patriotic in public. The ither twa whispered thegether, though, an' finally got up on a bench, lookin' awfu' solemn. They sang 'Ah've a Nigger Wench in Tiger Bay' tae a slow hymn-tune, an' the Dagoes stood at the salute richt

141

through the performance; there wis aboot twinty verses. Man, it wis fine tae see twa Britishers keepin' up the prestige o' their country in the face o' sich overwhelmin' odds, for the vino we had tae drink wasnae calculated tae bring inspiration to onybody but a Dago.

"Weel, there we were, a' square as ye micht say, though, if ye tak' volume intae accoont, we had them licked; the second mate had a voice that cairried frae the poop tae the fore to'-gallan' yaird in the teeth o' a gale.

"Anither drink or twa an' yin o' the Dagoes got busy wi' a gless an' a cork an' showed us some conjurin'. He followed it up wi' a few caird tricks, an' wance mair they looked at us wi' expectation. The situation wis fair desperate; nane o' us had a trick tae his name. Efter a consultation we decided on a grand finale, jist tae pit the lid on thae Dagoes wance an' for a' an' establish oor national superiority beyond a doot.

"The second mate, a great big red-heided son o' the Manse, got intae the middle o' the room; the wee third mate climbed on tae his shoulders an' stood there balancin' by the skin o' his teeth, wi' the second hangin' on tae his ankles like grim daith. Ma job wis tae haun' up yin' o' the chairs, an' he was gaun tae balance it on his chin. Wid he manage it? Think o' it, McNidder; it had become an affair o' national importance.

"The wee third mate got the chair up, inch by inch, an' lang afore it wis near his chin ma he'rt was in ma mooth. But he got it up, steadied it on his chin an' stretched oot his arms, jist like they dae on the stage.

" 'Viva!' yelled the wee Dago officers.

"That did it; the twa equileebrists swayed an' collapsed. The chair brained an admiring waiter, an' the third mate cam' doon wi' a rattle an' brought the chandelier as weel. It wis an awfu' wreck, but Britain's prestige wis secure.

"When we got things squared up we saw oor freens hame tae their barracks an' tried tae wish them Guid-nicht; but thae Latin races are naething if they're no' polite, so they turned oot the guard an' escorted us back tae the ship. Oor shipmates pit a wrang construction on that. But Ah'm telling ye the truth; it wis a guard o' honour an' no' the ither thing.

"Grub? Ay, we feed the country richt enough, McNidder, but individually an' quietly an' withoot ony trumpets the officer lads keep up oor prestige frae wan end o' the globe tae the ither, jist as Ah've been tellin' ye.

"An' that's whit the country owes tae the Merchant Service; but ye'll never read it in the papers."

Some Corner of a Foreign Glen

BILL TIDY on Scottish Expatriates

*"See, laddie. The same feeling as swingin'
through the trees without actually exerting
yourself!"*

"Och! For a minute I thought it was the Phantom Piper of the McDoons come for me!"

"C'mon, Rosita! Let's get married in the wee kirk o' the hill!"

144

"Hurry man! With a bit of luck I might just catch the Burmese and Thai New Years!"

"I'm surprised the US branch got visas for Tibet!"

"Golly, how super! Fancy meeting another English person here!"

Full Stop in the Dawdle from the North

"HERE'S a go," I said, turning to Sark, after carefully looking round the station to see if we really were back at Oban, having a quarter of an hour ago started (as we supposed) on our journey, already fifteen minutes late.

"Well, if you put it in that way," he said, "I should call it an entire absence of go. I thought it was a peculiarly jolting train. Never passed over so many points in the same time in my life."

"Looks as if we should miss train at Stirling," I remark, anxiously. "If so, we can't get on from Carlisle to Woodside to-night."

"Oh, that'll be all right," said Sark, airy to the last; "we'll make it up as we go along."

Again a sort of faint bluish light, which I had come to recognise as a smile, feebly flashed over cadaverous countenance of the stranger in corner seat.

Certainly no hurry in getting off. More whistling, more waving of green flag. Observed that natives who had come to see friends off had quietly waited on platform. Train evidently expected back. Now it had returned they said good-bye over again to friends. Train deliberately steams out of station thirty-five minutes late. Every eight or ten miles stopped at roadside station. No one got in or got out. After waiting five or six minutes, to see if any one would change his mind, train crawled out again. Performance repeated few miles further on with same result.

"Don't put your head out of the window and ask questions," Sark remonstrated, as I banged down the window. "I never did it since I heard a story against himself John Bright used to tell with great glee. Travelling homeward one day in a particularly slow train, it stopped an unconscionably long time at Oldham. Finally, losing all patience, he leaned out of the window, and in his most magisterial manner said, 'Is it intended that this train shall move on tonight?' The porter addressed, not knowing the great man, tartly replied, 'Put in thy big white yedd, and mebbe the train'll start.'"

Due at Loch Awe 1.32; half-past one when we strolled into Connel Ferry station, sixteen miles short of that point. Two more stations before we reach Loch Awe.

"Always heard it was a far cry to Loch Awe," said Sark, undauntedly determined to regard matters cheerfully.

"You haven't come to the hill yet," said a sepulchral voice in the corner.

"What hill?" I asked.

"Oh, you'll see soon enough. It's where we usually get out and walk. If there are on board the train any chums of the guard or driver, they are expected to lend a shoulder to help the train up."

Ice once broken, stranger became communicative. Told us his melancholy story. Had been a W. S. in Edinburgh. Five years ago, still in prime of life, bought a house at Oban; obliged to go to Edinburgh once, sometimes, twice, a week. Only thrice in all that time had train made junction with Edinburgh train at Stirling. Appetite failed; flesh fell away; spirits went down to water level. Through looking out of window on approaching Stirling, in hope of seeing South train waiting, eyes put on that gaze of strained anxiety that had puzzled me. Similarly habit contracted of involuntarily jerking up right hand with gesture designed to arrest departing train.

"Last week, coming north from Edinburgh," said the hapless passenger, "we were two hours late at Loch Awe. 'A little late to-day, aren't we?' I timidly observed to the guard. 'Ou aye! we're a bit late,' he said. 'Ye see, we had a lot of rams, and we couldna' get baith them and you up the hill; so we left ye at Tyndrum, and ran the rams through first, and then came back for ye.' "

Fifty minutes late at Killin Junction. So far from making up time lost at Oban, more lost at every wayside station. "I hope we shan't miss the train at Stirling?" I anxiously inquired of guard.

"Weel, no," said he, looking at his watch. "I dinna think ye'll hae managed that yet."

This spoken in soothing tones, warm from the kindly Scottish heart. Hadn't yet finally lost chance of missing train at Stirling that should enable us to keep our tryst at Woodside. But no need for despair. A little more dawdling and it would be done.

Done it was. When we reached Stirling, porters complacently announced English mail had left quarter of an hour ago. As for stationmaster, he was righteously indignant with inconsiderate travellers who showed disposition to lament their loss.

"Good night," said cadaverous fellow-passenger, feebly walking out of darkling station. "Hope you'll get a bed somewhere. Having been going up and down line for five years, I keep a bedroom close by. Cheaper in the end. I shall get on in the morning."

Tourist (landing on small island in Hebrides—to old resident). "Who lives here, my friend?"
"Oh, just me and the wife and my brither-in-law."
"And what sort of place is it?"
"Oh, an awfu' place for scandal."

THE ALL-CONQUERING SCOT

Old Scotsman (to his son, who has just returned from a business trip to London). "Weel, laddie, and what dae ye think o' the English noo?"
Son. "Oh, I didn't have much of a chance to study them. You see, I only had to do with the heads of departments!"

Tourist (to postmistress of small Scottish village). "Can I come inside out of the rain?"
Postmistress (suspiciously). "Do they let ye inside at Lunnon?"

How to Find a Scottish Ancestor

Would anyone interested in their Scottish origins please contact
E. S. TURNER, where they may learn something to their
advantage?

THE first question to ask yourself is: *Are you really sure you want to trace
your Scottish ancestry?* Are you ready for shocks?

Suppose your family line led inexorably to Sawney Bean, the Man-Eater of
Midlothian? Or to a mincing Ganymede at the Court of Holyrood?

Suppose it led to some kilted equivalent of the Jukes Family, a name to
frighten off amateur ancestor-hunters for life? (Jukes was a no-good settler in
America and a snap-check on 709 of his descendants revealed that 76 were
criminals, 128 prostitutes, 142 vagabonds and 131 blind, insane or infirm.
Jukes isn't the family's real name—but yours might be).

All right, so you'll take the risk—as Sir Robert Menzies, Thor Heyerdahl,
Sean Connery and James Robertson Justice have already done? You're not
afraid of being jostled in the lone shieling by searchers from Seattle or
Sacramento, arriving on special Ancestor Flights? Then the first step is to get in
touch with the admirable Scots Ancestry Research Society, which operates in a
Georgian eyrie in York Place, Edinburgh, overlooking an unusually fine
prospect of lums. This is a non-profit-making body, independent of public
funds, but with powerful friends in the Scots Establishment. Since it was
founded twenty-seven years ago it has handled 30,000 inquiries from persons of
Scots blood.

Tetchy Sassenachs will think it odd that such a body should exist at all. Why,
they will ask, set up a research institution for the mere gratifications of pride
and curiosity? Why not leave the field to the freelance tracers—men who
proclaim they will go anywhere, search anything? Anyway, why this world-
wide craze for unearthing and documenting Scots grandmothers? And why is
there not an *English* Ancestry Research Society?

Tetchy Sassenachs overlook the fact that there are about five times more
Scots overseas than there are in Scotland. It ill behoves the English, who helped
to stimulate the outflow of exiles, to object to a society which has the object of
binding the sons of those exiles more closely to their homeland. Price in Scots
blood can be a transfiguring joy, as anyone may see by inspecting a photograph
of Lord Thomson kilted out as Honorary Colonel of the Toronto Scottish.

The Scots Ancestry Research Society was founded in 1945, otherwise not one of the great founding years. It seems that the late Thomas Johnston, then Secretary of State for Scotland, was visiting Northwick Castle, Midlothian, where Scotland's records had been evacuated as a precaution against the Luftwaffe. There he was surprised to find several American servicemen diligently searching the registers for clues to their forebears. Already he had been impressed by the number of enquiries of this kind received by his Office. Why not, he argued, a professional body to assist the public with this worthy obsession?

With the help of like-minded, and impressively titled, citizens, including the Lord Lyon King of Arms, the Historiographer-Royal and the Keeper of the Records of Scotland, plus a donation of £1,000 from Lord Roseberry (whose horse, "Ocean Swell", won the Derby that year) the Society was launched. It had a thousand queries on its desk right away. Among these were requests for information about the antecedents of General Douglas MacArthur, America's Pacific supremo, whose grandfather was born in Glasgow, and of James McGill, founder of the Canadian university.

In England the quest for ancestors can involve a great deal of legwork, since the searcher must examine the parish records on the spot. In Scotland some 1,000 parish registers are concentrated in the New Register House, Edinburgh, where census information is also kept: an infinity of pride and embarrassment, meticulously stored. Ireland's records used to be conveniently massed too, but the rebels who set fire to the Four Courts in Dublin in 1922 destroyed the timber for a forest of family trees.

The Society's searchers are women graduates, full-time or part-time, whose enthusiasm has to be curbed by regulation: that is, they are not supposed to pore over difficult and faded handwriting for more than three hours at a time. It is a rule any union would approve. The fruits of their researches are confidential to the client, but he is free to boast about the findings as much as he likes. The cost is modest. At the outset he pays a non-returnable registration fee of two guineas and signs a form authorising the Society "to undertake research up to a maximum of twenty guineas (fifty-five dollars)." In practice the average fee charged is less than this. The fee covers only the paternal line, however; each additional line costs extra.

Most of the overseas inquiries come from America, though proportionally there are just as many from the Commonwealth. "We have successfully undertaken numerous searches for families whose ancestors emigrated during the Highland Clearances, but the upsets which followed the 'Forty-Five' present more difficulty," says Miss Patricia Baxendine, Director of the Society.

Of special fascination are the inquiries from persons whose Scots blood is mixed with Chinese, Fijian or Hawaiian. Those Scots ships' engineers fairly got around; and in Singapore and Honolulu, evidently, it is worth at least a postage stamp to find out more about them.

Each tourist season brings a new crop of callers to the Society's offices, more often men than women. Among them may be the occasional hopeful anxious to trace kinship with remote warrior heroes. Those seeking to establish claims to lands and titles are referred to the Lord Lyon King of Arms, an officer of the Scottish Household, who has his own court—and power to suppress heraldic impertinences.

In Scotland, as elsewhere, the best families have the best-kept records, some of them going back five or six centuries. Humbler lines are not too easy to trace beyond the mid-eighteenth century. Registration of births and deaths was not compulsory in Scotland until 1855, as against 1837 in England. Before that some of the parish registers were indifferently kept (a number of them are still unindexed). Records of Presbyterians tend to be more complete than those of Episcopalians and Catholics. The Isle of Skye—coveted ancestor country— had no parish registers before 1800.

Not every man with a clan name is necessarily descended from that clan; his forebears may have adopted the name, in days of persecution, for survival's sake. There was a time when the name of MacGregor was officially proscribed, those bearing it being deemed even more of a public nuisance than Jukeses. For facts about clans, septs and family ramifications, the searcher can apply to the non-commercial Scottish Tartans Society, at Broughty Castle, Broughty Ferry, Angus. (It may or may not recognise the Polaris Tartan designed for American Servicemen in Scotland some years ago.)

Ancestor-chasing would not be much fun if the search were confined to census rolls and parish registers. Scotland has its kirk records, from which it may appear that your ancestor was publicly rebuked, like Robert Burns, Jean Armour *et al,* for the sin of fornication. (An American professor is said to have been gratified to find that two of his direct ancestors had never married, since this was likely to make him seem a less illiberal figure in his family's eyes.) For the advanced researcher there are such archival bonuses as records of persons transported, lists of indentured servants packed off to America, muster rolls, bastardy rolls and works like Lancour's *Passenger Lists of Ships Coming To North America 1607–1825.*

The truly committed seeker will not be content with a many-branched chart for his wall. He will wish, like the folk from Seattle, to track down the old homestead, or what remains of it, to knock at lonely doors, to poke about in graveyards and even to wander thoughtfully in the heather where his kinsman indulged in the frolics to which he owes his existence. The hobby, as all must agree, is an educational one, it breaks no homes, it causes minimum inconvenience and it earns dollars for Britain.

And what a relief it must be to find that one's Scottish ancestors are, after all, the sort of people one would be happy, in due course, to be gathered unto.

Oh to be in Scotland!

McLACHLAN's hame thoughts frae abroad

"D'ye get many Scotch customers here?"
"No, Sir—can't complain."

The Great Scottish Myth

Is there any such thing as a Scotsman, or has he been invented by the English? HUGH MACPHERSON makes a border raid on the truth

I FIRST became aware of the Great Scottish Myth in a sewer beneath Clapham North tube station. It was the moment when head ganger Bill Brown—a Rabelaisian figure who would make Eliza Doolittle's dad seem a half-brother to Norman St. John-Stevas—said to me in mournful tones: "You know, Jock, there are people in London who treat their sewers like dustbins." I had been accepted.

Soon he was telling in hushed tones how Richard Dimbleby himself had been in the very same sewer. (Certainly the brickwork looked like a Victorian cathedral.) Then a fellow clansman, one McKenzie from Jamaica, who was the colour of Cadbury's cocoa, began to bang the iron ladder by which we had descended. It was the sign that rain was falling and he was anxious that the sewers of London should not foam with our blood. We went upstairs to the van for a cup of tea. Bill Brown ordered: "Show him the pictures." A magazine was then produced from beneath a seat replete with lusty naked ladies such as adorn the walls of Transport House clutching railway trains and ships. I must confess that my taste in nubile womanhood runs slightly nearer Twiggy than Tessie O'Shea, but I was touched. For I am quite sure of one thing. He did not show them to Richard Dimbleby.

With the passing of time I grew to appreciate the value of the Myth even more. There was the accountant who listened to me speak and said: "He's just like Doctor Cameron." Now Andrew Cruickshank is a fine old Aberdonian, domiciled in SW1, who has lived among the English for more than forty years. He is a prominent member of the Church of England, and cohabits (televisually) with an Irish lady to portray Scots of the 'twenties, as conceived by a proud Caledonian currently resident in Lucerne, Switzerland. I bear as much resemblance to Dr. Cameron as I do to William Rees-Mogg. But clearly such is the value of the Myth that the Scot abroad can be pressed into any particular fantasy role the Anglo-Saxon might want to place him. Poor but proud; educated, classless, couthy and reliable. The intrepid ship's engineer; the grumpy brilliant doctor; the classless civil service mogul. The really wise Caledonian realises this at an early age and gratefully lives off it for the rest of his life.

157

When a suitably weighty study is made of this extraordinary phenomenon, a proud place will be reserved for that celebrated Scottish Mythman, Harold Macmillan. Although I always saw him as akin to some long-suffering uncle of Bertie Wooster who went into politics, he would in fact from time to time refer to himself as "a crofter's grandson." Truth to tell his grandfather came from the Ayrshire town of Irvine where crofts are as thick on the ground as igloos. Grandad Daniel was indeed poor, as were his other more remote ancestors. But Highland poverty had a certain sanctity. The Great Myth decrees that it is linked with honest endeavour, a thirst for knowledge and the approval of the Almighty. Could anyone in their right senses imagine Harold Macmillan wipe a tear from his eye and refer to his poor grandad who sold whelks at Wigan Pier? (We know who *would* but that's another story). A treasured memory is of him, then the Minister of Housing, seated by a tiled fireplace at the Ideal Homes Exhibition, amidst furniture typical of the parlours of plebeian England— luxurious beyond the dreams of his remote crofter ancestors. He looks as comfortable as the Pope on a pastoral call at the home of the Rev. Ian Paisley. The Myth is not only powerful but classless. It is of the same value to upper-crust Englishmen of distant Scottish ancestry as to the working class Gael.

Of course if it were all stern resolve and sanctified poverty it would be a dreadful bore—and appalling for the tourist industry. In fact what was needed to spice the brew was a touch of romanticism. If tartan-laden Rob Roy McGregors did not exist the English would have invented them. Actually they didn't have to. It was done for them by Sir Walter Scott who has anaesthetised more schoolboys with his books than his Edinburgh contemporary Sir James Simpson did with his chloroform.

Now whatever one may think of Sir Walter as a novelist, when it came to knocking out Highland garments, to produce a romantic Celtic setting for the visit of George IV to Edinburgh in 1822, he put the Caernarvon team of Snowdon and Norfolk in the shade. Such was his success that in latter days he might even have merited a profile in the *New Statesman* ("The author's children actually wear trews designed by Sir Walter . . .") Not only did Sir Walter clamber into a Campbell tartan kilt, not only did he persuade sixty-three peers and seventy-seven baronets to swan around like characters from his novels; not only did no less a person than the Lord Mayor of London appear garbed in a tartan creation the like of which was not seen again till the 1947 New York production of *Brigadoon,* but George IV himself turned up in a Stewart tartan kilt. Truth to tell the king did spoil the effect a little by wearing long silk tights as undergarments. But from that day every Royal primate, above the level of a corgi, who puts foot across the border, is promptly slapped into Highland Dress. The fact that 99·99 per cent of home Scots would as soon be seen in a kilt as Mr. Malcolm Muggeridge would in the Playboy Club has not made the slightest difference to the romantic nonsense invented by Scott. The Great Scottish Myth has been enriched—as have generations of Edinburgh tartan rug manufacturers.

Every myth must, of course, have some flickers of reality. There was a time I suppose when the Scots were on the average better educated than the English, even if that has been reversed in the last decade. What is more, to enjoy the benefits of the Myth the Scots themselves have to indulge in a little self-deception. Take the poet Robert Burns, beloved of Caledonian Societies and visiting Russian delegations, for whom he is as inseparable a companion to Dickens as Flanagan is to Allen, or Burke is to Hare. The sad fact, as the greatest contemporary Scottish poet Hugh MacDiarmid once bewailed, is that Scots know about as much of his work as the average Englishman. I imagine that means the first verse of *Auld Lang Syne* and the start of "Wee, sleekit, cow'rin', tim'rous beastie . . ." But few would admit this sad fact.

A memory I will cherish till the day I meet my Maker (who, I am sure, will look something like Lord Reith) is of a certain Glasgow minister conducting morning service in a school gymnasium. For reasons of obscure spiritual origin, he elected to recite the whole of *Tam O' Shanter,* which is the account of a drunken night culminating in a tangle with a witches' Sabbath. (Actually it was suspected that he was rehearsing for a regimental Burns's Supper). Suddenly he woke the entire staff by grinding to a halt in the middle. He appealed to the headmaster for help to no avail. Desperately he turned to the English Department, proud products of the much-vaunted Scottish educational system, who were seated solemnly in a row on a bench. He might as well have asked for an original quotation from the Koran.

Be that as it may I am the last to despise the Great Myth. I owe it too much. At the drop of a hat I can slip into one of the many roles of the Scot abroad: the earthiness of Sir Alec Douglas Home; the cheeriness of Fyfe Robertson; the sophistication of Sir Harry Lauder. People will trust me as they did Ramsay MacDonald, and the fact that I am a fellow spirit of Lord Reith will be the open sesame to every trendy party up the King's Road. And wherever I travel in the world I will care not if the English start a club and exclude the local natives. It will be a matter of total indifference to me that the Welsh start choirs and the Irish start fights. I will join the local Caledonian Society.

LIFE IN SCOTLAND

A company director who was suspected of stealing car doors drove across fields when he was followed because he thought someone was trying to rob him. *(Edinburgh Evening News)*

Mr. Mark Steiner, depute-fiscal, said, "It was quite clear that the accused lacked the civility and courtesy of police officers. He also did not have the demeanour and dignity of CID officers. Indeed, he is employed with the Scottish Gas Board." *(Dundee Evening Telegraph)*

HE

END